*Masters of Equitation
on Counter-canter and
Flying Changes*

# Masters of Equitation on Counter-canter and Flying Changes

Compiled by
## Martin Diggle

J. A. Allen
London

J.A. Allen
Clerkenwell House, Clerkenwell Green, London EC1R 0HT

J.A. Allen is an imprint of Robert Hale Ltd

*British Library Cataloguing in Publication Data*
A catalogue record for this book is available from the British Library

All extracts from *Dressage a Guidebook for the Road to Success* by Alfred Knopfhart are reproduced by permission of Half Halt Press, Inc. (PO Box 67, Boonsboro, Maryland 21756, USA), from *Dressage A Study of the Finer Points of Riding* by Henry Wynmalen by permission of the Wilshire Book Company (California, USA), from *The Complete Training of Horse and Rider* by Alois Podhajsky by permission of The Sportsman's Press; from *The Gymnasium of the Horse* by Gustav Steinbrecht by permission of Xenophon Press (Cleveland Heights, Ohio, USA).

The following photographs and illustrations are also reproduced by permission: Counter-canter – cantering left on the right rein (page 20), Faulty counter-canter (page 31), Simple change of canter (page 51), Flying change from right to left (page 92), Incorrect flying change; split change in left canter (page 100) and Incorrect flying change (page 102) from Knopfhart's *Dressage A Guidebook for the Road to Success* by permission of Half Halt Press, Inc. (PO Box 67, Boonsboro, Maryland 21756, USA); The moment of suspension (page 59) and the photo sequence on pages 116–7 from Paul Belasik's *Dressage for the 21st Century* by permission of Karl Leck; Change of lead to near fore (page 74) from Henry Wynmalen's *Dressage A Study of the Finer Points of Riding* by permission of the Wilshire Book Company (California USA).

Jacket photograph of the compiler by permission of Mike Freeman

Design by Nancy Lawrence
Series compiler Martin Diggle
Colour separation by Tenon & Polert Colour Scanning Ltd
Printed in Singapore by Kyodo Printing Co (S'pore) Pte Ltd

# Contents

*Introduction to the Masters of Equitation Series* 7

*Compiler's Note* 11

*Introduction to the Masters of Equitation on*
 *Counter-canter and Flying Changes* 13

Counter-canter 15
 Purposes of Counter-canter 15
 Preparation 24
 Introduction and Practice 26

Flying Changes 38
 Historical Development 39
 Preparation for the Changes 47
 Mechanics of the Flying Change 55
 The Rider's Aids 65
 Introducing the Single Change 77
 Faults in the Change 97
 Developing Sequence Changes 108

*Conclusion* 118
*Bibliography* 120
*Biographies of Quoted Masters* 123

# Introduction to the Masters of Equitation on Dressage Series

When we first discover a new pursuit, most of us explore it with more enthusiasm than science. This is necessarily so, since our desire to participate greatly exceeds our understanding of the principles involved. It is when we begin actively to seek a greater understanding of these principles that we can be sure that we have acquired a genuine new interest, and are not simply indulging a passing fad.

In our quest for knowledge, we look first to the nearest and most obvious sources. If our new interest is riding, we acquire an instructor, listen (hopefully) to what we are told, and begin to question the apparent paradoxes of equitation as they unfold. With time, our field of information broadens; we learn what our instructor has been told by his or her instructor, we begin to follow the exploits of top riders in the different disciplines, and we even start to read books.

It is at some point along this path that we start to realise just what a wealth of knowledge we have at our disposal. We also begin to realise that much of this knowledge is far from new. There is initial surprise when we learn that the elderly gentleman who trains our current idol was, himself, an Olympic medallist – a further surprise that he, in turn, was trained by a cavalry officer famed, in his time, as a leading light of the Cadre Noir. We discover in a book written forty or fifty years ago ideas of which we were unaware, and then marvel at the extensive references to writers long dead before the author's own birth. We regard, with awe, faded, grainy photographs of riders whose positions – even to our untutored eyes – look positively centaur-like, and we are bemused by ancient diagrams of school movements that make today's dressage tests seem like a hack in the park.

If, at this point, we pause to reflect a little, we start to see this heritage in its true context. It is a common human conceit to believe that we, or our near contemporaries, are the first to discover anything, but this is very rarely true. So far as riding is concerned, it is no exaggeration to say that it is, in absolute terms, less important to us than it was to our ancestors. If we need to prove this point we can consider that, three hundred years ago, a poorly ridden lateral movement might result in decapitation by an enemy sabre. The same movement, ridden today, would result in an 'insufficient' on the test sheet, and a wounded ego.

Of course, not all equitation historically was concerned with the vital necessities of war. Certainly since the Renaissance, there have always been people fascinated by the art of riding – interestingly, this group includes a number of Masters who were, first and foremost, military men.

It is in the nature of art to give birth to experimentation, innovation and re-interpretation, and it is in the nature of artists to be influenced by – even to borrow from – others, and yet still develop their own styles. Sometimes, in pursuit of new ideas, an acknowledged Master may stray too far down a particular path, causing even his most admiring pupils to question the wisdom of the route, but such instances have a way of triggering the reassessment and consolidation of major principles.

All of these things have happened in equitation, against a background of different types and breeds of horses, and varying equestrian requirements. Not surprisingly, this has given rise to a number of schools, or philosophies, which place different degrees of emphasis on certain principles. By delving into the wealth of literature available, it is possible for the avid reader to discover these philosophies, and draw from them ideas and information which may be of personal value. However, because of the volume of material available, and the need to embark upon a major voyage of discovery, this can be considered an extensive – albeit rewarding – process.

The purpose behind the *Masters of Equitation* series is to gather together, under individual subject headings, many of the key thoughts of eminent equestrians, thus providing a convenient source of reference to their ideas. The reader is invited to research, compare and contrast – and may find a special significance in areas of obvious consensus.

# *Compiler's Note*

In producing this series of books, the aims of the publisher are twofold. First, it is certainly the intention that they should act as reference works, giving readers with specific schooling queries access to the thoughts of many Masters in a single volume.

Second, it is very much hoped that they will act as an appetiser, a stimulus for further reading of the original works cited and, indeed, for Classical equestrian works in general.

With regard to this latter aim, I can foresee that some readers, who have already made a study of the Classics, may search this book in vain for their favourite extract or author. If this happens, I beg such readers' pardon. The truth is, in order to be completely comprehensive, a book such as this would have to quote great swathes of material from very many sources – an undertaking that would exhaust the energies of compiler, publisher and perhaps even the most ardent reader! Furthermore, so far as the flying change is concerned, this is a complex movement that is widely acknowledged to present different problems with different horses. Consequently, many authorities address the training of the movement, and the specific difficulties encountered, in considerable depth. While I have endeavoured to provide a useful sample of the relevant material, it would, in many cases, be inappropriate to quote it in its entirety in what is essentially a book of extracts.

What I have endeavoured to do in this whole series is to provide a good cross-section of references from different eras, countries and schools of equestrian thought. It was, indeed, the publisher's express wish that the series should contain a broad overview of various ideas and persuasions and that it should not seek to promote the ideas of one School over another.

Regarding the matter of eras, however, I should mention that most of the authorities quoted in this book are relatively modern, by which I mean mainly nineteenth century onward. This is not because of any disrespect for the old Masters of the Renaissance period; it simply reflects the subject matter of this book. Although the old Masters used counter-canter, they did so almost exclusively for its pragmatic value (to straighten crookedness), and had relatively little to say on the subject. They did not, for example, use it as a preparation for flying changes, for the simple reason that they did not apparently practise that exercise. Scholars of Classical equitation have, so far, been unable to find evidence that the flying change was practised deliberately until well into the nineteenth century, and the development of the one-time changes is generally attributed to the enigmatic François Baucher, who died in 1873.

However, Classical equitation is a layered process, not only in terms of training strategy, but also in the sense that each generation of riders has the opportunity to build upon the work of preceding generations. Most of the true Masters of each generation pay tribute to the work of those who preceded them, not only in terms of lip service but also in their equestrian practice. Therefore, even though the majority of authorities quoted in this book are relatively recent, the reader will discover that the older Masters are well represented both in spirit and in principle.

# Introduction to the Masters of Equitation on Counter-canter and Flying Changes

The counter-canter and flying change are both progressions of the basic canter and although there is a clear relationship between them they have distinct derivations and purposes. While the counter-canter is a long-established exercise, the flying change is a relatively new addition to the list of classically accepted movements. As with so much in equitation, it is essential that both exercises are introduced at an appropriate stage in the horse's training, and that the purposes and aims are clearly understood. To these ends, this book examines the derivation and uses of the counter-canter, and the complexities surrounding the introduction and execution of flying changes, through the eyes of various Masters. It is hoped that their thoughts will assist those who wish to advance their horses' education in the gait of canter.

For the benefit of any readers unfamiliar with the usage, I feel I should repeat the point made in the introduction to *Masters of Equitation on Canter*, which is that many European writers have traditionally used the French *galop* (which serves for both canter and gallop) when referring to the three-beat gait of canter. This, in many instances, has been rendered as 'gallop' in translations – some examples of which appear in the following pages.

One other issue that might require clarification is the use of the terms 'inside' and 'outside' in the context of counter-canter.

When a horse is in counter-canter he will generally be flexed slightly in the direction of his leading leg (for example, flexed slightly to the left when counter-cantering in a right-hand direction). In this context, the terms 'inside' and 'outside' are commonly employed *with reference to the horse's bend* rather than with reference to the arena. Thus, in the example given, the horse's (and the rider's) 'inside' will be the left, that is, the side actually to the *outside* of the arena. (Please note, however, that where reference reverts to the *arena*, 'inside' and 'outside' will convey their usual meanings of 'nearer the centre' and 'nearer the wall' respectively.) In some of the extracts relating to counter-canter quoted in this book, this point is made clear by the author; in some, it will be apparent from the context. In other cases, however, the reader's knowledge of this convention may be assumed by the author concerned. I hope that this note will serve to prevent any possible confusion in such cases.

# Counter-canter

An enquiring mind and a capacity for observing the actions of others are invaluable tools in any field of study. So, indeed, is an ability to analyse and question one's own actions and intentions. Therefore, as we begin to study the Masters' thoughts on counter-canter, we might legitimately ask the question: 'Why ride counter-canter at all?' After all, the mechanics of canter are such that there is a natural correlation between the horse's leading leg and the direction in which he is moving – so why change this? Why not simply ask for left lead if we wish to move to the left, and vice versa? Considered in juxtaposition with flying changes, this question may seem even more pertinent. If we intend to develop the horse's natural capacity to change lead in a moment, 'in the air', why should we not do this from the outset, rather than requiring him to canter for periods 'on the wrong leg'? These are the first questions about which we should seek clarification from the Masters.

## Purposes of Counter-canter

It might be useful to begin with a summary of the practical value of both counter-canter and flying changes by the twentieth century Master, Richard Wätjen:

A horse who has learned to move without difficulty at the counter-canter...and to execute the flying change of leg willingly...will not only have great advantages in the arena as a dressage horse, but also as a show jumper and hunter through increased suppleness and obedience.

The suppleness of the dressage horse will be greatly increased by the collected counter-canter, whereby lowering of the croup and an increased bending of the hocks will be achieved. The horse learns to obey willingly the aids of the rider, thus reaching a higher degree of obedience. Show jumpers, which are well trained at the counter-canter and execute properly the flying change...are much handier when jumping a course, and they can be ridden at a fast pace even at sharp turns and short approaches...                    Richard Wätjen *Dressage Riding*

Wätjen's emphasis on showjumping is undoubtedly related to his own success in that discipline, but this passage also serves to highlight the part that hunting and jumping played historically in the development of the movements under discussion. To demonstrate this further, here is that great Master and innovator, de la Guérinière, observing a lesson from the hunting field:

I have seen knowledgeable men use an excellent lesson for hunting horses, which is to gallop them on a large circle on the left rein while holding the horse curved slightly to the right and united on the right leg. This turning to the left while travelling on the right leg teaches the horse not to become disunited when changing direction...

François Robichon de la Guérinière *School of Horsemanship*

While it suggests recognition of the suppling and balancing roles of counter-canter, this extract raises two points. The first is a very basic question. Why, as a general principle, was it *required* that hunters should counter-canter in this fashion – why did they not simply canter on the left lead when going left? The answer appears to lie in a deep-seated convention that hunters cantered habitually on the right lead. In a passage extolling the use of shoulder-in as a remedy for crookedness in canter, de la Guérinière writes:

This fault...can easily be seen in the case of most gallops, e.g. on the right leg, which is the way hunting and work horses gallop.

François Robichon de la Guérinière *School of Horsemanship*

There is evidence that this convention was long-lasting. As recently as the end of the nineteenth century, James Fillis, whose own riding was heavily influenced by the French School of the nineteenth century, wrote:

On a straight line in the open we generally canter with the off fore leading...
James Fillis *Breaking and Riding*

The existence of this convention pretty much answers the second question invited by de la Guérinière's observation: why did the hunters not change lead – perhaps by flying changes? However, there is a supplementary answer to this, which is that, as deliberate practice, the flying change was unknown in de la Guérinière's day – a point that will be considered further when flying changes are discussed.

If we return to de la Guérinière's mention of crookedness, it is here that we find the fundamental rationale for counter-canter. This is summarised by the contemporary authority, Paul Belasik:

As we have seen, most horses are not straight in the dressage sense, which means that the sides of the horse will not be

17

symmetrical. In one direction the horse will be softer and will have a tendency to bend easily, or even too much. In the other direction the horse's body will feel stiff. Over the years, there have been many opinions as to which side is the problem side. It seems fair to say that, today, we appreciate the interconnected nature of the horse's body and understand that most problems are dual. If a horse is too stiff to the left, it is usually too soft to the right, and vice versa. In the basic canter, one of the most difficult tasks is to make the asymmetrical horse straight: very often the horse will canter fairly straight on its stiff side, but carry its haunches crooked to the inside on its softer side.

The importance of correcting this fault is recognized by all factions of riding, and the attempts to correct it run the whole gamut of methods. However, one of the oldest methods, which originates from riding in a school or a building with walls, is the counter-canter. When the old masters encountered a horse that carried its haunches to the inside, away from the wall and towards the middle of the arena, they simply reversed the direction of travel and rode the problem canter in the other direction. Now the wall trapped the escaping haunches. As the rider practiced this exercise with the horse's body molded by the wall, the crooked true canter was made straight by riding it in a counter-direction, hence the name counter-canter.

Paul Belasik  *Dressage for the 21st Century*

**The basic premise here is highlighted by this advice from Üdo Burger:**

The main difficulty is the right canter lead in which most horses have a tendency to hold the croup to the right. The best way to obviate this is to do a counter-canter on the left circle (right lead) until the horse assumes of his own accord a correct inflexion…  Üdo Burger  *The Way to Perfect Horsemanship*

**And a similar observation by Waldemar Seunig:**

The usefulness of brief rides at the counter-gallop to make the outside leg (which plays the principal part at the gallop) more supple was pointed out earlier in the discussion of galloping. The counter-gallop is also an excellent remedy for crookedness, which will make its appearance more or less seriously whenever new demands are made of the horse.

Waldemar Seunig Horsemanship

**The pragmatic value of counter-canter is discussed in unequivocal tones by Alfred Knopfhart:**

The fact is that as a gait the counter-canter is of no utilitarian value. It is purely gymnastic work...designed to improve the maneuverability of the horse. In this respect, its unquestionable advantages were recognized many hundreds of years ago, and it has for that reason become firmly established in our system of training and in the FEI tests.

Of what particular advantage then is the counter-canter compared to other work at canter?

Nobody denies the necessity of teaching horses to move straight when loaded with the weight of a rider, especially at the canter. For this reason, the counter-canter is of invaluable assistance. Since the inside of the horse is then turned towards the wall of the arena, the sideways evasion of the inside hind, often so difficult to prevent in true canter, is more difficult. That is provided, of course, the movement is correctly ridden, with the horse's inside shoulder closer to the wall than his inside hip...

It is this position, which must be carefully maintained especially in the corners, that deprives the horse of the possibility of cantering crookedly by turning his hindquarters in. The rider's outside leg (relative to position) counters any tendency to turn

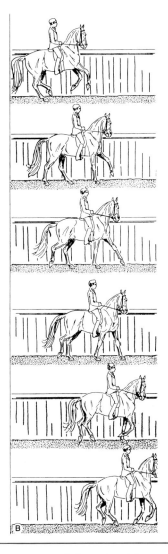

*Counter-canter – cantering left on the right rein – from Alfred Knopfhart's* Dressage A Guidebook for the Road to Success.

the quarters out.

When the counter-canter is executed along the wall, the outside rein can be more effectively used to keep the neck straight since the presence of the wall obviates the evasion of the hindquarters which most horses resort to in true canter in order to avoid uncomfortable flexion of the inside hind.

Alfred Knopfhart  *Dressage A Guidebook for the Road to Success*

**The relative positioning of the horse's inside shoulder mentioned by Knopfhart is also referred to by Seunig:**

The counter gallop becomes especially valuable when the horse's shoulders are carefully guided, the forehand always being turned towards the wall ahead of the inside hind foot. The inside hind leg near the wall can be better controlled and supervised in the false gallop than in the corresponding simple gallop. This will naturally have a favourable effect on the activity of the outside hind foot and thus improve the horse's entire posture.

Waldemar Seunig  *Horsemanship*

**After discussing the role of counter-canter in alleviating crookedness, Knopfhart goes on to explain the relationship between this function and the development of collection:**

Besides this, the counter-canter can also be used to improve collection. This, in fact, is its principal purpose.

It is known that collection cannot be enhanced unless one can succeed in shortening the convex side of the horse. In the counter-canter as the hindquarter is turned outwards when turning, the task of the outside rein becomes much facilitated...

The counter-canter, which was invented, practiced and developed by the creative riding masters of the past, has never failed in its purpose when used with tact and understanding.

Alfred Knopfhart  *Dressage A Guidebook for the Road to Success*

**The role of counter-canter in straightening and collecting is also emphasised by Nuno Oliveira…**

Counter canter is an extremely efficacious procedure in dressage training, and is an extraordinary preparation for the collected canter. If it is done on the outside track of the riding school, the wall will stop the croup from escaping, preventing the horse from refusing to flex the inside hind leg…by making a barrier against the lateral displacement of the croup.

The rider can pay attention in the regular canter to the maintenance and flexion of the inside hind leg, as he has the wall to control the outside hind leg. More attention should be paid to the outside hind leg (according to the canter) in the counter canter whose activity favours at the same time that of the inside hind leg.

We can cadence the gait, activate it, make it rounder, and transform it into a canter with greatly superior impulsion by means of the counter canter, without fear of making the horse crooked.

**…who goes on to mention the contribution that this work can make to increasing flexibility and strength:**

The horse's collection will be activated and perfected by the counter canter…

It is the counter canter which gives mobility to the croup, by activating the hind legs…

When circles in counter canter are started, the croup pushes the horse's body energetically because of the position of the two hind legs, which are necessarily flexed and activated strongly.

Activation of the inside hind leg (in accordance with the canter) which is accentuated by the counter canter, will make the start of voltes, haunches in, much more simple later on, as well as normal pirouettes, as it is the inside hind leg which must be bent the most in order to bear the horse's mass pivoting around it.

In summary, he quotes the nineteenth century German Master, Gustav Steinbrecht:

'The counter canter will assure us of a decisive strength in the horse.' (Steinbrecht)          Nuno Oliveira  *Reflections on Equestrian Art*

Oliveira's comprehensive list of the benefits of counter-canter, supplemented by the thoughts of the other Masters, should convince us that the counter-canter is far more than just preparatory work for the flying change. The fact that it does have this function, among others, is pointed out in simple terms by Alois Podhajsky...

The *counter canter* must be practised when preparing for the flying change... It is also an effective means of straightening a horse that has a tendency to go crooked.

    Alois Podhajsky  *The Complete Training of Horse and Rider*

...and Erik Herbermann:

Counter-canter is both a collecting exercise, excellent for suppling, and a preparatory exercise for flying changes of lead.

            Erik Herbermann  *Dressage Formula*

While Henry Wynmalen adds an important message that developing the horse's understanding must go hand in glove with developing his physical powers:

The counterlead, or false canter, fulfils two purposes.

In the first place it is the means to make the horse understand that he is never to change his leading leg except upon the rider's implicit instructions. As such it is an absolutely indispensable preparation before the changes of leg in the air...are attempted.

In the second place it is a powerful suppling exercise, since it requires the horse to find his balance in a mode of progression which he would not use normally, entailing the use of muscles in unusual combinations...

Henry Wynmalen *Dressage A Study of the Finer Points of Riding*

## *Preparation*

**Background preparation and choosing the right time to begin the work are key factors in the successful introduction of all ridden exercises. So far as counter-canter is concerned, it is a basic premise that it cannot be introduced until the true canter is established to a reasonable level.**

The counter-canter, to be of any value, already requires the horse to carry itself well in the canter.

Gustav Steinbrecht *The Gymnasium of the Horse*

Before starting with the 'counter-canter' the horse must be...properly balanced at the shortened canter.

Richard Wätjen *Dressage Riding*

Many riders wonder when they can start teaching the horse to counter-canter. The answer is that several conditions must be fulfilled...

To begin with, the horse must have learned to canter true, in horizontal equilibrium, on all the figures required in novice and elementary tests. The working canter should have become really active and perfectly regular, and it should be possible to obtain a few slightly collected strides. Correct execution of what can be described as an active, slightly shortened working canter of…figures…involving turns…would be a good test of sufficient submission and suppleness. If the horse remains calm, secure and regular in turns and on straight lines to both hands, the rider may safely ask for a change of hand using counter-canter.

The counter-canter, in fact, should not cause any problem if the horse has been well prepared in work at the true canter.

Alfred Knopfhart  *Dressage A Guidebook for the Road to Success*

**In two sentences, the French Olympic rider André Jousseaume both reiterates key benefits of the counter-canter, and puts the preparatory work in context.**

…As soon as the horse performs these [10m] circles correctly, without being heavy on the hand…the time has come to begin the counter canter.

It is a good idea to begin the counter canter as soon as possible, because it is an excellent suppling exercise and, by giving more work to the difficult side, both sides can finally be made about equal.  André Jousseaume  *Progressive Dressage*

**In other words, while he is keen to begin the counter-canter as soon as possible, his concept of what this entails is a true canter of sufficient balance and lightness that the horse can perform 10m circles with accuracy and ease.**

**If the Masters warn us to make proper preparation for new work, they also warn that the work should be introduced with discretion. Here, Oliveira and Steinbrecht warn both against being overdemanding and insufficiently aware of the quality of work.**

Counter canter is an extraordinary method by which the hind legs can be activated at the canter, but care is needed to ensure that the horse does not become over tired at first as it is a violent exercise for him...

It must not be overdone, as then instead of having a beneficial effect, it will come to have a harmful one.

Counter canter, above all in the corners, is difficult at first for many horses. If, at the corner, the horse changes lead, leans toward the inside [of the school], or becomes disunited, he should be stopped and collected in order to strike off again in counter canter.         Nuno Oliveira  *Reflections on Equestrian Art*

If thus the counter-canter gives us greater power over the horse, it also harbors the danger of misuse for the inexperienced rider and it should therefore again be pointed out that the correctness of the work should always be checked through pace and contact. Here, as in all exercises which require very energetic activity from the horse, one should not forget to carefully adapt the length of the sessions to the capability of the horse and at any time better make them too short than too long.

Gustav Steinbrecht  *The Gymnasium of the Horse*

## *Introduction and Practice*

The horse is generally introduced to the idea of counter-canter via shallow loops or extended demi-voltes. While the Masters tend toward individual preferences in this respect, the concept of progressive work remains universal. The progression of intro-ductory exercises favoured by André Jousseaume is as follows:

The preparation for the counter canter is carried out by doing slight counter changes of hand the whole length of the long side…

At first, move one or two metres away from the track, start the counter change of hand at the beginning of the long side, and ride a diagonal line, very gradually going away from the track until the centre line is reached, which marks the change of direction to be made. This change of direction must be performed quietly to avoid a change of lead or, which is more frequent, that the horse canters disunited. If necessary, flatten out the angle of the counter change of hand by cantering parallel to the long side for a few metres. In this case, the change of direction will be made in two stages, which makes it possible to avoid changing leads with horses showing some difficulties when commencing this exercise. It should be noted that this difficulty is generally encountered on one side only of the horse. The outside leg…watches over the haunches and intervenes rapidly should there be an attempt to change leads.

After developing exercises based on the counter change of hand, Jousseaume recommends:

Counter canter on large circles, progressively decreasing the diameter…according to the horse's progress. [Then…]

On the figure eight. Excellent suppling exercise, the horse going alternately from the inside lead on one circle to a counter canter on the other circle.

He then underscores the importance of this progressive approach with a highly significant comment:

This work should not present any serious difficulties if the progression has been followed correctly, doing each exercise on both hands. If, when going on to the next stage of training, difficulties are too great, it must be deduced that the rider wanted to go too fast. In this case, return to the preceding exercises and improve them. André Jousseaume  *Progressive Dressage*

**Alfred Knopfhart shows a marked similarity to Jousseaume, both in terms of the progression of exercises prescribed, and in the counsel of measured, patient progress:**

Regarding progression, one must start with the easiest exercise, which does not entail a change of bend. This is a very shallow loop on the long side, so shallow that the horse does not feel that he is in fact counter-cantering on the second part of the loop. If the horse has been properly prepared he will remain quite unperturbed. It may be possible, perhaps even in the course of the first lesson, to make the curve more pronounced. In any case, after no more than a few days it should be possible to execute the more pronounced change of direction with equal facility on both hands. After this, one can progress to the figure eight and then to the complete circle and the serpentine...

It is, of course, impossible to state the length of time needed before one can progress from one form of the exercise to the next more difficult one. It depends entirely on the behavior of the horse. If he maintains calmness, regularity and unaltered equilibrium in the counter-canter, after one or two circles or turns one should go back to true canter. If, on the contrary, he starts to hurry or lean on the hand, a transition to walk must be immediately executed to get the horse sufficiently collected. One then returns to a controlled true canter with a few turns and voltes to improve carriage and suppleness before once again with due prudence giving the horse a short and simple lesson in counter-canter.

Alfred Knopfhart  *Dressage A Guidebook for the Road to Success*

Here are the thoughts of two authorities, James Fillis and Richard Wätjen, who favoured using demi-voltes to introduce counter-canter. In addition to emphasising steady progress in the introductory stage, it seems evident that Fillis views this work as a step in improving the horse's obedience and laying groundwork for the flying changes:

When the horse can do demi-voltes well, I prolong them for some strides at the canter, without changing the leg. Thus, I begin the demi-volte at the wall, which is on my left. While cantering the horse with the off fore leading, I turn to the right, and continue to keep up the canter on the off fore, even after the demi-volte, but only during two or three strides at the first attempt. I increase the number of these strides only little by little, according to the lightness and cleverness of the horse. This is the most simple way to teach a horse to canter with the right leg when turning to the left; and *vice versa.* This exercise is indispensable if we wish to readily obtain changes of leg when cantering round to the right or left.

When the horse goes round the school correctly on the leg which is next to the wall, we should start several times with the off fore leading, and also with the near fore leading, both to the right and to the left, while always keeping him along the wall

James Fillis  *Breaking and Riding*

While Richard Wätjen puts a good deal of emphasis on the rider's responsibility to apply the aids correctly:

By a turn in the corner of the long side of the arena *(demi volte)* the rider can easily execute the 'counter-canter'. The horse must, of course, be kept between the rider's seat, legs and reins...The inside leg (at the counter-canter now the outside one) maintains the canter, whereas the inside rein gives the horse – exactly as at the true canter – the direction. The corners have to be – especially at the beginning – well rounded, and the impulsion has to be increased in passing the corners, so that the horse properly learns to engage its hocks. If a horse changes leg or breaks against the rider's will, the exercise has to be repeated by a stronger influence of the outside rein and outside leg, and not by force or the use of the spur. The same applies in cantering through the corners. It is advisable to change again into the true canter by changing the rein in order to avoid the change on the track, otherwise the horse which is not so well trained easily gets into the habit of freeing itself out of the counter-canter by a flying change…At the beginning, a slight sideways position (as at the *Renvers*) may be allowed, but gradually the horse must canter in a correct head and neck position on one track. Richard Wätjen *Dressage Riding*

It is interesting to note that, in describing the applications of the aids, Wätjen uses moderate terms such as 'support' and 'maintain' and, even when he refers to 'stronger influences' he proscribes the use of force. The following extract from Knopfhart's *Dressage A Guidebook for the Road to Success*, which deals with rider faults in counter-canter, contains some elements which, superficially, appear to contradict some of the points made by Wätjen. A closer comparison may suggest that, whereas Wätjen is talking of the rider dealing with, or accommodating, initial flaws in the work, Knopfhart is warning against clumsy, exaggerated aids which might *induce* these flaws.

It must be said that almost always when a horse hurries in counter-canter it is because an inexperienced rider in his efforts to prevent a change of lead, urges the horse on with exaggeratedly strong aids, especially with that of his outside leg, sits much too heavily, exaggerates the lateral weight effect or, alternately, sits on the wrong side.

Strong pressure of the outside leg is useless in preventing a break of the canter to the trot; on the contrary, it often provokes the break because it can result in forcing the horse to move on two tracks. A relatively uneducated horse cannot possibly remain in counter-canter on two tracks.

Leaning in the direction of the turn is equally detrimental. If, for example, the horse is in right canter to the left hand…the rider must sit to the right, and it is the inside, right hind of the horse, rather than the left hind, that he must activate mostly. If the inside right hind steps outwards towards the outside of the turn (probably because of excessive pressure from the rider's left [outside] leg), the horse is given all liberty to disrupt the counter-canter. It is partly with the inside leg and partly with the reins that one prevents this from happening.

Alfred Knopfhart  *Dressage A Guidebook for the Road to Success*

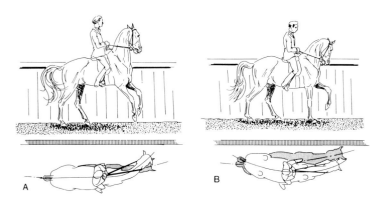

*Faulty counter-canter.*  **A** = *Active elevation of the neck, hollowing of the back, impure sequence of footfalls.*  **B** = *Excessively restraining hands, horse overbent, canter over-shortened.*

*Faulty counter-canter, from Alfred Knopfhart's*  Dressage A Guidebook for the Road to Success.

The theme of the rider's aids, and due attention to the underlying principles, is taken up by Alois Podhajsky (who here uses 'inside' and 'outside' with reference to the *arena*, rather than the horse's bend):

In the counter canter the rider will employ the opposite aids to those for the correct canter. The inside leg behind the girth announces the movement, while the outside leg demands the strike-off, creates the bend to the outside, and ensures the smooth rhythm of the movement. The outside rein leads the horse along the wall, and is responsible for the correct position of the horse's head to the outside, preventing the shoulder from being brought in and the canter from becoming crooked. The inside rein limits the position to the outside and helps the outside rein in directing the horse...

When first practising the counter canter it is advisable to describe a large arc when going through the corner and to increase the tempo slightly to make it easier for the horse.

Alois Podhajsky  *The Complete Training of Horse and Rider*

Waldemar Seunig also emphasises the need for plenty of impulsion and easy turns at first.

The rider must be particularly attentive to the curvature of the horse during the turns...which at first must not be taken too close or too tight, and that the even, fluid three beat of the stride is maintained. Therefore see that the impulsion has been developed before the turn, since even perfectly aligned hindquarters must describe a somewhat larger circle and canter against the normal flexion, which modifies the horse's impulsion. By means of a lightly controlling hand on the outside rein which lightens the horse's forehand supported by driving aids which alternate tactfully with the rein effects, the rider thus maintains the impulsion and the roundness of the canter which would otherwise be lost in the positioning of the turn and result in the horse stumbling into a dull and dragging four beat.

In the course of further schooling at the counter canter, the hocks will become ever more flexible and strong, the counter canter turns ever more fluent and balanced. The previously necessary and often supervisory controlling aid of the outside leg to prevent the change of lead can be eliminated, and the harmonious distribution of weight will become habit.

Waldemar Seunig  *The Essence of Horsemanship*

As well as being a motivating force in British dressage, Henry Wynmalen was a lifelong enthusiast for cross-country riding, and a long time Master of Foxhounds. It is no surprise that his preferred method of introducing the counter-canter involved a large field. The following extract from *Dressage A Study of the Finer Points of Riding* highlights Wynmalen's underlying determination to see things from the horse's point of view and create a real understanding between horse and rider. Another advocate of measured progression, he places great emphasis on patient explanation and offers a very practical warning against giving the horse unpleasant memories.

In the ordinary way of nature the horse will assume the canter to the right, or to the left, or change from one to the other in accordance with his natural balance and his natural judgment. [In his other work, *Equitation,* Wynmalen develops this theme with the observation that: When entering a turn with, in his perfectly justified opinion, the wrong leg leading, every semi-schooled horse will automatically change the leading leg. So, in fact, will the well schooled horse, but only so long as we give him no indication to the contrary!]

Instead, we now want him to understand that he must give up acting in accordance with his own sense of balance and that he must in future submit to our judgment in the matter.

We have the means to do this...since the horse is already thoroughly familiar with our aids for the canter and is obedient to them under normal conditions. But we have now to obtain this obedience under the abnormal conditions of the counterlead also.

It is not difficult to succeed in this at the appropriate stage of the horse's training, but it does require tact; it is...an exercise in which we can only succeed by explaining to the horse's brain and not by acting forcibly on his anatomy.

We need plenty of room to begin this exercise. Let us assume that we are going round a sizeable field in an anti-clockwise direction. We strike-off at the canter with the off-fore leading at

*Circle at the canter, counterlead, from Henry Wynmalen's* Equitation.

the beginning of a long straight line. We sit quite still, keeping the horse quietly but markedly on the aids; we are careful in particular to maintain the feel on the right rein...We then begin a very faint curve to the left. We do that by using the left rein, quite carefully, as direct or opening rein; but without changing our aids for the right canter or our position in the saddle.

If the curve is slight enough, that should cause no difficulty. We continue this exercise by forming the curved line into a [faint] serpentine; we ride this serpentine without changing leg, so that the horse is alternately cantering true and false.

These are, for the reasons already stated, difficult exercises for the horse...it will take time to develop these faint serpentines into more defined serpentines, into circles and figures of eight without change of leg.

It also means that the horse will frequently change leg of his own accord; he may do a true change or change only in front and continue disunited. When this happens we bring our horse gently back to a walk, walk a few strides and strike-off again, equally gently, on the required leg.

The accent here is decidedly on 'gently'! We are 'explaining' to our horse. If we use punishment, roughness, or even impatience...the horse will conclude that it is wrong to change, under any circumstances, and that to do so leads to unpleasant consequences. The horse never forgets. So, once that conclusion has become fixed in his mind, we shall meet with considerable difficulties when it comes to obtaining changes on demand.

Henry Wynmalen *Dressage A Study of the Finer Points of Riding*

**Wynmalen may be in a minority when he says that:**

To derive the full benefit of this exercise, and to do it correctly in the long run, the horse, when false cantering on a circle ...should be able to bend over his whole length round the rider's inside leg, whilst maintaining a flexion in the mouth to the outside rein. Thus, when describing a circle to the left at the counterlead, with the off-fore leading, the horse's body and neck shall be bent in conformity with the circular track; precisely as would be correct for the true canter, but with the exception of a right flexion of the mouth, maintained by the outside rein.

Henry Wynmalen  *Dressage A Study of the Finer Points of Riding*

Here are the views of two other authorities on the issue of bend:

At the counter-canter the horse leads with its outside [of the arena] front leg…The horse should always be bent in the direction of the leading leg.  Erik Herbermann  *Dressage Formula*

On a circle in counter-canter, a horse cannot be bent along the line of the circumference; he has to remain slightly bent around the rider's inside leg [in terms of the canter lead], and thus bent, he follows the curvature of the circle. Constant even bend must be maintained, and the haunches must not be allowed to drift to the rider's inside. Most of all, it is imperative to maintain rhythm, tempo and impulsion…The counter-canter is…a very useful exercise to develop flexion and thrust of the horse's outside hind leg, which is so important to canter work.

John Winnett  *Dressage as Art in Competition*

It is possible, however, that Wynmalen's intentions are similar to those of Jousseaume, who describes the more advanced work at counter-canter in these terms:

Work at the counter canter must be done on circles of progressively smaller diameter, as well as on the figure of eight.

Pay attention to the following points:

1. Be sure to keep the bend to the correct side (*placer** to the right for the canter to the right).

2. As training progresses and when the horse does a counter canter with no contraction whatsoever, try to mould the horse around the curve, that is, seek a light curving of the spinal column *while maintaining the placer* on the correct side. The horse then gives the feeling of bending slightly around the rider's leg, which is on the inside of the circle.

As a rule, this result will not be obtained until the end of training when the horse is supple at a slow canter, with no contraction and perfectly light.

*placer might be defined as a very slight lateral bend of the neck, accompanied by a slight yielding to the rein on the same side.

André Jousseaume  Progressive Dressage

Whatever the level of acceptance for Wynmalen's and Jousseaume's views on bend, it seems indisputable that their aims are to achieve the highest possible degrees of suppleness and balance. These aims sit squarely with Oliveira's contention that:

The horse which is not capable of maintaining the correct lead in any position, or in any circumstance, cannot be said to be sufficiently in submission.

Nuno Oliveira  Reflections on Equestrian Art

Perhaps the last word on this subject should be left to Podhajsky, who wrote:

The movement of the counter canter must be just as smooth as that of the correct canter…A good counter canter with active bounds, with the hind legs following the tracks of the forelegs and no change in the tempo, will be an excellent proof of the suppleness of the horse, especially as he passes through the corners…

Alois Podhajsky  The Complete Training of Horse and Rider

# *Flying Changes*

At the beginning of the section on counter-canter, we asked the question: 'If we are going to teach the horse flying changes, why do we need counter-canter?' Our new question, the corollary to the first one, must be: 'Why ride flying changes?' If the horse can achieve the levels of balance and suppleness in counter-canter which the Masters prescribe as ideals, why bother with the complex process of changing lead 'in the air'?

Before dismissing this question as naïve, or as posturing logic at odds with practicality, we should perhaps consider this point. From the Renaissance period onward, for several centuries, the old Masters – who laid the ground rules for classical equitation – explored and practised a huge variety of complex movements. There is no discernible evidence that these movements included the flying change.

In an exploration of the most suitable aids for true canter, Henry Wynmalen, a great student of Classical equitation wrote:

The ancient masters were quite unconcerned about cantering somewhat sideways; in fact they delighted so much in cantering on two tracks that they were going sideways most of the time anyway.

But, and this is the quintessence of the matter, they did not practise the changes of leg! And, to obtain satisfactory changes of leg, especially at short intervals, the horse must canter straight.

Henry Wynmalen *Dressage A Study of the Finer Points of Riding*

**Another student of the classics, Paul Belasik, stated that:**

Flying changes at every stride, in fact even single flying changes, were not practised (as far as I have been able to determine) in the baroque days of la Guérinière.

Paul Belasik *Riding Towards the Light*

**More than a decade later, he confirms this view, reiterating:**

Although there were many lateral exercises practiced in earlier times, there is, to my knowledge, no mention of flying changes until well into the nineteenth century. Certainly, multiple flying changes are not mentioned before this time. It seems that the introduction of deliberate, multiple, repeated changes as an exercise began in that era, and credit for one-time changes (a flying change every stride), is usually given to the French circus rider, François Baucher.

Paul Belasik *Dressage for the 21st Century*

## *Historical Development*

Although there may be hints as to why the old Masters did not perform flying changes – preoccupation with lateral work and the convention of right lead in the open, for example – a definitive reason is hard to find. Perhaps the nearest we come to discovering one is in Decarpentry's *Academic Equitation*. Having written…

To allow the horse to change behind first without difficulty, as he must always do, his quarters must be very free, and therefore considerably unloaded.

...the author adds this footnote:

It is for this reason that ticklish mares that buck in resistance to the rider's leg change the lead only too readily. It is also why the 'change in the air' – which we practise frequently – was considered by the old masters to be a difficult movement. Their horses were considerably more 'on their haunches' than ours, and the overloading of the hindquarters made the leap of the hind legs, which permits the change, difficult. The old masters practised particularly a 'two-time' change, also called 'de ferme a ferme' (i.e. with a transition to and from the halt).

General Decarpentry *Academic Equitation*

A historical change in the extent to which the hindquarters were habitually loaded, and in the horse's overall balance, are factors noted by Paul Belasik. Exploring reasons for the introduction of the flying change, and its increase in popularity, he writes:

If, in terms of the horse's gaits, there is one area of expertise where the modern horseman could feel confident in comparison with the old masters, it is in the canter. In the last hundred years or so, the work in the canter, more than any other gait, has shown the most notable changes. Oddly enough, the classical dressage schools cannot really take the credit for initiating the advances in the canter, even though they have perfected them. The understanding and development of the new exercises for the canter came from three main areas in the late nineteenth and early twentieth centuries – jumping, racing and the circus (not necessarily in that order of precedence).

After the dissolution of the French monarchy and the school of Versailles, equestrian field sports became increasingly popular. Hunting, and with it jumping and racing, began an ascendancy that continued into the twentieth century.

In the early years of that century, it was Federico Caprilli's revolutionary jumping style that changed the face of riding. His work was often a direct reproof aimed at high school dressage. A very strong case can be made that it was because of Caprilli's new ideas about balance, and freedom for the horse's neck, that dressage changed…Furthermore, almost all of Caprilli's ideas were developed in the canter, the gait most widely used for the popular outdoor sports, in which changes of direction obviously occurred. It is a certainty that flying changes were deliberately practiced then…

Finally, in the continuous pushing of novelty to the limits, circus riders like François Baucher and James Fillis tried to do everything to the canter. Much of this work…was held in disdain by dressage purists, because it seemed too far removed from what came naturally to the horse. However, it was very difficult to continue to argue that multiple flying changes were also unnatural. Flying changes were and are exhibited by free horses all the time, even in multiples…

Paul Belasik *Dressage for the 21st Century*

While Belasik is correct in describing both Baucher and Fillis as circus riders – and while it is true that Fillis practised some strange variations of canter – it is also the case that Fillis had a wider remit than Baucher, of whom he was, in his earlier career, a disciple. Unlike Baucher, who was almost exclusively a school rider, Fillis practised a wide range of exterior disciplines. The rapid acceptance of the flying change (at least in its single form) is chronicled in his comment, at the end of the nineteenth century, that:

…the rider should… also know how to make the horse *change his leg*, namely, to pass from one canter into the other canter

41

without stopping. This is not high school work, but belongs to ordinary riding, whether practised in the school or outside...

James Fillis *Breaking and Riding*

Where Belasik mentions Baucher elsewhere in his writing, he uses the term 'controversial' – a view that is widely shared. General Decarpentry – a great equestrian thinker, but not, himself, immune from controversy – was a grandson of a pupil of Baucher's. However, his own influences were quite broad-based, and he was by no means a slavish disciple of Baucher. His view on the background to Baucher's development of tempi changes must be of considerable interest:

Decarpentry said of Baucher that he brought to the movements of the horse: 'an exactitude and a correctness that the schools of the past never had *(Baucher et son Ecole)*. This exactitude enabled Baucher to accomplish movements that previous equerries had never been able to do, for example, changes of leg at each beat of the gallop...

Hilda Nelson *François Baucher The Man and his Method*

Coupling the concept of 'exactitude and correctness' with Baucher's legacy of controversy leads us into an era of protracted debate. Certainly, single changes were readily absorbed into what Fillis called 'ordinary riding', and doubtless Belasik is correct to cite the influence of disciplines other than dressage in this respect. (Indeed, the practical advantages of the single change for hunters and jumpers are highlighted in the extract from Wätjen's *Dressage Riding*, which was used to introduce the earlier section on counter-canter.) Also, although some authorities questioned the intrinsic value of sequence changes, and their order of precedence in the programme of classical exercises, there was little resistance to them as a general concept, since most agreed, as Belasik writes, that horses at liberty might exhibit multiple changes. The sticking point, the crux of the controversy, was the acceptance of the one-time changes as 'natural'. The overview on these issues is expressed here by Waldemar Seunig:

We often see horses whose training is not quite complete executing fairly good changes of lead at every stride. All this confirms us in the belief that correctly executed changes...*à tempo* are far from the most convincing touchstone of complete gymnastic training despite the high factors assigned to them in the present Olympic dressage tests. They are, to be sure, proof of dexterity, impulsion and responsiveness, based on fairly advanced dressage. Nor can we reject the opinion out of hand that the changes of lead after four, three, and two gallops belong to the secondary field school and the *haute école*, because the natural gallop leap is expressed at least once between each change. We do reject, however, the change of lead at each stride as being artificiality rather than an art, in which the picture of the natural gallop is distorted.

Although we sometimes see unbroken horses executing passages, pirouettes, caprioles, and several successive changes of lead at the gallop down to only two strides, flying changes at every stride will hardly be attempted by a foal no matter how pliant and enterprising it is.        Waldemar Seunig *Horsemanship*

The debate on one-time changes even raged inside the Spanish Riding School:

Throughout the history of riding there have been bitter and inconclusive arguments as to which movements are really natural to the horse. Alois Podhajsky...has written that such debates went on inside the citadel of classical equitation, the great

Spanish Riding School, itself. Flying changes at every stride…have been such a debatable movement… Podhajsky once stated that the question of flying changes at every stride had never been resolved in Vienna, yet today they are accepted and are universally performed and exhibited even at that same school.                    Paul Belasik  *Riding Towards the Light*

**Podhajsky's own view, which has marked similarities to those of Seunig, is given in *The Complete Training of Horse and Rider*. After stating that…**

Changing the leading leg after a certain number of strides, especially in one-time, may be considered among the most spectacular of exercises and tempt the rider to practise it more than necessary, although its value in training is relatively small. Flying changes can be performed with less collection and less suppleness, whereas pirouettes, passage and piaffe will never succeed without the maximum of these qualities.

**…he goes on to say:**

*Changes at every stride* are one of the most controversial exercises as a number of experts consider them circus movements and disapprove of them for this reason. Many arguments took place at the Spanish Riding School, without ever coming to a satisfactory conclusion. No one could give a reasonable explanation either for or against them. But the Fédération Equestre Internationale, as the ruling body on international equitation, declares that they belong to the classical exercises and demands them in the dressage tests at the Olympic Games. It is, therefore, superfluous to discuss the matter in this book.

Alois Podhajsky  *The Complete Training of Horse and Rider*

The last two sentences here suggest that Podhajsky, who was both a guardian of classical equitation and an active international competitor, may have been in something of a cleft stick on this issue. In his book *My Horses, My Teachers*, he tells the following anecdote, which throws much light upon the initial impact that one-time changes had on the competitive world.

In the autumn of 1933...Nora had...mastered all exercises... demanded in the Grand Prix...except the flying change of lead at every stride. This...was disapproved of by the Director of the Spanish Riding School in those days because he proclaimed that it did not count among the exercises of classical equitation. Consequently I had not learned it during my attendance at the School. I hesitated to ask General von Pongràcz to teach these one-time changes to Nora because so far I had trained my horse all by myself...I remembered, however, that the general had told me some time ago that on the occasion of the Olympic Games in 1928 the...Hungarian team had come to Amsterdam without being able to perform changes from stride to stride, which were on the programme for the first time, because they assumed that the riders of the other nations would not be capable of executing this 'unnatural' movement either. Much to their surprise they discovered that almost all the other participants performed this disputable flying change. In this plight the captain of the Hungarian team...turned to him for advice and asked him how to teach this air to a horse. 'Oh, this is very simple', was the answer. 'You strike off into the canter right and into the canter left and you go on repeating this until the horse performs a change from stride to stride'...

This story came to my mind when I found myself in a similar plight...For some time I practised a great deal of canter, striking off frequently and alternating the canter left and right. I shortened the intervals between the strike-offs more and more until one day Nora performed two successive changes. Overjoyed, I dismounted on the spot, rewarded her lavishly…and sent her back into the stables. On the following day, I repeated the exercise with the same result and the same reward. On the third day, when I struck off into the canter Nora performed immediately two perfect changes from stride to stride. Now I knew she had understood but this time I did not send her back into the stables because she had to become used to executing these changes at every stride upon my command and then continue her work. Alois Podhajsky *My Horses, My Teachers*

**Things have moved on since the 1930s, and the one-time changes are now more or less universally accepted – at least, on a pragmatic level. John Winnett was brought up in France, and his early equestrian education was heavily influenced by the French academic tradition of Saumur. Subsequently, he studied with leading figures in Germany, including Reiner Klimke. For almost two whole decades, the 1970s and 1980s, he represented the USA with conspicuous success at the highest levels of international competition. Here are his thoughts on the subject:**

I often wonder whether the exercise of flying changes at every stride is art or circus! Certainly, we do not see horses at play in the field changing leads at every stride. Surely, the skipping rhythm of the gait does nothing to improve the horse's canter. Considering the emphasis the F.E.I. places on flying changes at every stride in their tests, we must assume that they become the proof of the rider's dexterity and the horse's responsiveness. John Winnett *Dressage as Art in Competition*

**…it may be that the underlying principles are still subject to debate.**

## *Preparation for the Changes*

As in all lessons, but particularly in the change of lead, we must not allow our animated, willing horse to become prejudiced against the new exercise. This would inevitably follow if we went at it without calm preparation and instruction, endeavouring to squeeze a flying change out of it as soon as possible by energetic use of the spurs and rein controls. A horse that has undergone such forcible exercising will never learn how to execute a change of lead with willing devotion to forward movement...such a horse will...execute the change with ears laid back, stumbling, holding back, and with a high croup, even if the phase sequence of its steps is correct.            Waldemar Seunig *Horsemanship*

**There is little doubt that all discerning riders would heed Seunig's counsel for proper preparation, but what precisely does this entail? We have already seen that one use of counter-canter is as preparation for the changes, but what are the overall qualities required by the Masters before flying changes are introduced into the training programme?**

We should exercise great care in teaching the horse to change his leg...the proper time is when he has become free, supple, light, and well balanced in all his paces, obedient, and above all things, attentive to the 'aids'...            James Fillis *Breaking and Riding*

The horse must be well impulsioned, and well cadenced at a canter in three beats time, and he must hold himself straight on each hand (this is the most difficult thing for a horse) before he starts to do flying changes or pirouettes.

Nuno Oliveira  *Notes and Reminiscences of a Portuguese Rider*

---

A fluent flying change is inconceivable in the absence of impulsion...

    Alfred Knopfhart   *Dressage A Guidebook for the Road to Success*

Before one starts practising the flying change the horse has to be absolutely firm in striking off on the proper leg, and has to respond to the slightest aid of the rider's inside leg. A horse which is really light and sensitive to these inside leg-aids will not have great difficulty in learning the flying change. The rider should start with this exercise only when his horse is absolutely supple and obedient on the *straight line* and in all turns and other figures...Only an *absolutely straight horse* which has reached a higher degree of collection, *without pushing sideways against the rider's legs* is sufficiently advanced in its dressage training to be taught the correct 'flying change'. It is important that a dressage horse should only be taught this 'flying change' at the collected canter, whereas the show jumper and cross-country horse should not be trained at a shortened canter, but should advance with long strides...with longer reins and a lower head and neck position. A shortening of the neck and swinging sideways has to be avoided at all times...     Richard Wätjen   *Dressage Riding*

As the flying change takes place in the moment of suspension, the horse should not be asked to attempt it until he is fully balanced and the hindquarters are strong enough for him to spring actively off the ground...

    Alois Podhajsky   *The Complete Training of Horse and Rider*

**Podhajsky expands upon the importance of strength and impulsion, and explains that a lack of these qualities can cause further problems:**

With Kunz I learned that the flying change is developed from a correct canter, that is, from a lively canter in which the hind legs jump well under the body of the horse…If the rider insists on beginning with flying changes before this condition is met, his work will be far more difficult and besides many faults will appear which later will be hard to correct or eliminate. In most cases the horse will become crooked or not jump a full stride with his hind legs or not in the same rhythm with his forelegs. Instead of performing the change in a smooth forward bound he will execute it nearly on the spot; this gives the impression of hopping clumsily and is also most uncomfortable for the rider.

Alois Podhajsky  *My Horses, My Teachers*

**Podhajsky also recounts a cautionary tale which emphasises the importance of making the horse as straight as possible before teaching the flying changes – and the importance, to even a great rider, of having 'eyes on the ground'.**

As Maestoso Flora's training proceeded…I prepared him for the flying changes by frequent strike-offs into the canter on both reins from the trot and the walk. This preparation, in fact, enabled him to perform the flying change to the right at the first attempt. It took a little longer to obtain it to the left side because, like humans, horses are usually stronger or more adept on one side than on the other. When the change of lead to the left side finally succeeded, I made the mistake of not having it checked immediately by my faithful Flasar. A few days later I noticed that Maestoso Flora did not jump with the hind legs under his body as completely when changing to the left as when changing to the right. His movements were so smooth, however, that I was unable to feel the fault. Once more I remembered the advice of the old General von Pongràcz that the rider's work needs to be controlled constantly. It took a much longer time to correct this fault than to teach the exercise originally because I had to begin all over again…       Alois Podhajsky  *My Horses, My Teachers*

One exercise that is widely used in preparation for the flying change is the simple change, in which the canter lead is changed via a few transitional steps of walk. It seems that the enigmatic Baucher initially rode simple changes through halt, from which he proceeded directly to the flying change...

Passing frequently from a gallop with the right foot to that with the left, in a straight line, and with halts, will soon bring the horse to make these changes of feet by the touch without halting. Violent effects of force should be avoided, which would bewilder the horse and destroy his lightness. We must remember that this lightness which should precede all changes of pace and direction, and make every movement easy, graceful and inevitable, is the important condition we should seek before everything else.

François Baucher  *New Method of Horsemanship* in *François Baucher the Man and his Method by* Hilda Nelson

...but this is not a method that has been widely followed. Waldemar Seunig describes a more familiar simple change through walk:

Once the carriage of the horse at the false gallop presents no difficulties, we can start exercising the simple change of lead at the gallop. To do this, the rider changes to the walk, changes his seat and the horse's position, and departs at the gallop on the other lead after a few steps, depending upon the dexterity of the horse. This important transition, the smooth and fluent execution of which is a prerequisite for the flying change, can be readily performed at the stage of training now attained.

Waldemar Seunig  *Horsemanship*

Seunig advised introducing the flying change, via the simple change, once counter-canter had been established. While he

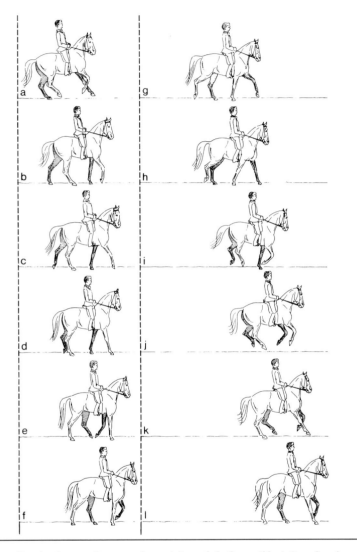

*Simple change of canter, from right to left, from Alfred Knopfhart's*
Dressage A Guidebook for the Road to Success.

recognised that some talented horses could, in fact, be taught the movement at an earlier stage, he warned that this practice risked introducing flaws that would cause problems as the work advanced.

Animated horses of good conformation can be trained for the flying change of lead even earlier. They rapidly grow accustomed to the controls that restrain one side and invite the other to advance, soon meeting their riders half-way with changes of lead that are apparently faultless. We still believe, however, that a horse called upon to perform the flying change of lead only when it is completely responsive and in hand will be able to overcome the subsequent difficulties of several flying changes of lead in succession much more easily than a 'prodigy', which has grown accustomed to idiosyncrasies and distortions because changes of lead were premature and hence not sufficiently precise. Waldemar Seunig *Horsemanship*

**The following passage suggests that John Winnett agrees with Seunig that, while some horses can be taught flying changes at an exceptionally early stage, it is usually better to wait until certain qualities are established. However, he also has an interesting observation to make regarding the possible effects of great suppleness upon straightness:**

I have found through experience that it is best to wait until the horse has reached a high degree of suppleness, strength and self-carriage. In certain cases, when a horse has a very good canter and shows talent for flying changes, I start to teach them earlier, before he has reached a high degree of suppleness. At this stage, a horse will perform straighter changes initially than later when he becomes very supple.

John Winnett *Dressage as Art in Competition*

It is evident from the text that this is not a warning against *obtaining* great suppleness. Rather, it is the pragmatic remark of an experienced practitioner. This pragmatism is also evident in Knopfhart's advice to treat horses as individuals and 'hasten slowly':

One should start to teach the flying change as soon as the horse feels perfectly balanced in counter-canter. 'Never rush, but do not tarry' is the motto of the intelligent trainer.

Teaching a horse to execute a flying change should never be done before he can canter straight in perfect horizontal equilibrium, can be evenly bent on voltes to both hands, and is perfectly submissive to the aids. Horses vary so much in their aptitudes and disposition that it is impossible to say how long it may take to achieve this result, but it is certainly not obtainable within a matter of weeks or months from the beginning of schooling…

Alfred Knopfhart *Dressage A Guidebook for the Road to Success*

If we refer back to the Masters' thoughts on counter-canter itself, we will note that Knopfhart's reference to perfect balance indicates not only the horse's ability to counter-canter, but also the presence of other desirable qualities of training. The intelligent trainer will always develop these qualities, and utilise individual exercises, in ways that are complementary to each other. Here, Paul Belasik makes a point similar in principle to that of John Winnett that, however valuable an exercise or quality may be in context, over-emphasising it can be counterproductive in terms of progress:

Although the counter-canter plays an important part in the preparation for flying changes, I now know not to wait too long before beginning to train them. Early in my career, I religiously heeded the advice of my teachers to make sure that the counter-canter was confirmed before attempting the flying changes; and too often the counter-canter became too concrete – so confirmed that it was difficult to get the horse out of it.

Paul Belasik  *Dressage for the 21st Century*

In a similar vein, Podhajsky warns of the need to attune the horse to precise aids, to retain his attention, and to avoid working in a way that might engender anticipation:

When the rider is satisfied that sufficient progress has been made, he will demand alternating correct and 'false' canter on the straight line…in order to teach his horse to answer the most delicate aids. On any suspicion of anticipation the rider must change the order of his exercises, using his imagination to ensure that the horse executes only what is required of him.

Alois Podhajsky  *The Complete Training of Horse and Rider*

Looking ahead a little, to when the horse has been introduced to the flying change, Podhajsky develops this theme. Here, he makes a point which is a mirror image of the one made by Belasik. Whereas Belasik is concerned that a horse who is over-established in the counter-canter may see no need to change lead, Podhajsky warns that work on changes may compromise the horse's desire to counter-canter, and thus advises practising both exercises in tandem. Essentially, both authorities are warning against practising one exercise to an extent that is detrimental to another.

As soon as the horse understands the flying change, the change should be alternated with the counter canter when passing through corners to ensure obedience to the aids especially with horses that are inclined to change of their own accord.

Alois Podhajsky  *The Complete Training of Horse and Rider*

## Mechanics of the Flying Change

John Winnett provides a concise definition of what flying changes are, and how they should be performed.

Flying changes are nothing more than canter departs in the air. To be correct and artistic, the change must be very straight and springing forward with impulsion and expression. The hind legs must come through almost to the line of maximum thrust. The shoulders must be supple, allowing the forelegs forward extended expression.       John Winnett *Dressage as Art in Competition*

It might be appropriate to follow John Winnett's concise definition of what flying changes are, and how they should be performed, with this, as it were, idealised picture from Henry Wynmalen. Wynmalen is making reference to the ease with which a horse at liberty can perform the movement, the aim being to replicate this ease in the ridden horse.

The change is called 'in the air' because the horse, not hindered, does the change during the…brief moment when he has all four legs off the ground. During this minute fraction of a second, he reverses the relative position of all his limbs. He does that with such unfailing accuracy and smoothness that the action is barely discernible in the saddle and has no effect whatever on the rider's comfortable adhesion. He does it without acceleration or deceleration; the rhythm of the canter is undisturbed; it is merely the lead which changes; he does it perfectly straight and without any need to swing…

He then proceeds to make a crucial point:

---

The purity, or otherwise, of the change...is determined by the change of the initiating hindleg...if that fails, everything fails!

Henry Wynmalen  *Dressage A Study of the Finer Points of Riding*

That great technician, Nuno Oliveira, describes the mechanics of the change:

It is necessary to make a complete study of strike offs at the canter, practising them from the walk and from halts in order to completely understand and execute correct flying changes.

During the normal flying change, the inversion of the natural disposition of the hind legs begins as the inside fore leg is put down, and finishes during the time of suspension. The inversion of the fore legs' normal disposition begins during the time of suspension, continuing on during the descent and placing of the outside hind leg. For example, in the canter to the right, the legs go down in the following order: left hind leg, left diagonal, right fore leg.

At the moment when the right hind leg is put down, marking the first beat of the canter on the left lead, the flying change of the hind legs should occur.

The left hind leg should prolong its support, and its placement depends upon that of its neighbour. The succession in the placement of the legs...constitutes the left canter: right hind leg, right diagonal, left fore leg.    Nuno Oliveira  *Reflections on Equestrian Art*

This brings us to the crucial issue – the timing of the aids, which is universally agreed to be of fundamental importance. There is also a consensus among the Masters that it is necessary to apply the aids somewhat earlier than the phase of suspension, although the precise timing stipulated may vary a little. André Jousseaume recommends 'slightly before the third phase':

It is obvious that the change of lead should not be demanded at just any phase of the canter stride. There is a time when it is

*The sequence of footfalls at canter, from Ulrik Schramm's* The Undisciplined Horse.

easier for the horse to carry it out. This instant must be seized, if immediate action is desired, and this will be very important when close successive changes...are reached.

The third phase of the canter is the most favourable, because, at this time, only one foreleg is grounded, while the other three legs are in the air. Thus, they are in a favourable situation to be prepared to modify the succession of footfalls, and the following phase, which is the phase of suspension, will allow the horse to prepare his new stride. Taking into account the fraction of a second necessary for the rider's indications to be transmitted to the horse's leg...the rider's demand should be made slightly before the third phase. The...rider should develop an instinctive feeling for the footfalls, so that he may act with precision...

André Jousseaume  *Progressive Dressage*

**Others prefer a fractionally earlier aid, favouring the moment when the principal diagonal is grounded:**

In order to understand more about the flying change, it is necessary to understand the sequence of the canter stride before, during and after the change. Once the horse's inner foreleg has pushed off after the third beat of the canter, the phase of suspension follows, during which he must change his lead to prevent the outside hind leg from taking its load first. Since it did up to now, greater load must be put on the leg that was formerly the inside leg, making it touch down earlier. The other leg, now carrying the same weight, swings forward for a longer time and alights later, so that the two hind legs have interchanged their roles. The flying change is initiated by the hind legs and finishes with the forelegs... The aids must be applied as soon as the principal diagonal is grounded and not wait until the time of suspension – which would be too late.

John Winnett  *Dressage as Art in Competition*

*The moment of suspension, from Paul Belasik's* Dressage for the 21st Century.

The change of leg should be required only at a certain period of the stride, when it is easiest for the horse to do...The best time to obtain the change of leg is at the fourth period, because the horse is then in the air. To obtain the change of leg during the fourth period, we should give the signal to the horse during the second period, when the diagonal is in support.

James Fillis *Breaking and Riding*

Once the horse's inner forefoot has pushed off after the third beat of the gallop, the phase of suspension follows, during which it must change its lead. To keep the outside hind foot from taking the load first, as it did up to now, greater load must be put on the leg that was formerly the inside leg, making it alight earlier.

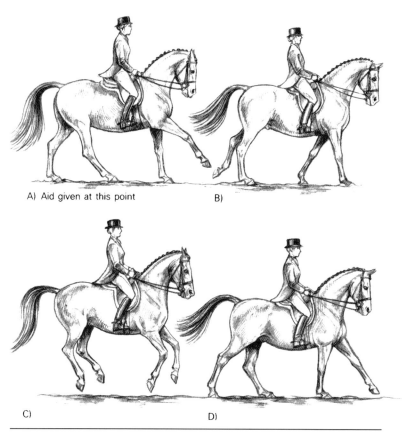

A) Aid given at this point   B)

C)   D)

*Timing the aids for the flying change, as illustrated in John Winnett's* Dressage as Art in Competition.

*(i) The moment of change from left to right.*

*(ii) Change to canter right.*

*Flying changes – the moment of transition, from John Winnett's* Dressage as Art in Competition.

The other (now carrying a smaller load) swings forward for a longer time and alights later, so that the two hind legs have interchanged their roles.

The rider's controls must therefore act to facilitate this change, which of course involves also the horse's forelegs. Guidance and seat must 'frame' the horse during this change in such a way that its only forward alternative is swinging into the new gallop...

It is often said that the prescribed leg and rein controls should be exercised while the horse is in the phase of suspension. This is the most unproductive kind of theorizing. If we do that while training a young horse we will always be too late. As we have said, the controls must be applied as soon as the principal diagonal is grounded!  Waldemar Seunig *Horsemanship*

The rider's second difficulty is to select the correct moment at which to give the aids. That moment must precede the execution of the movement by some time-lapse...sufficient...to leave the horse time to obey our order when next he is in the air...Precisely how long this time-lapse should be cannot be stated; it depends to some extent on the quickness of the horse's reactions and therefore on his experience...

By way of general guidance, I advise to apply the aids... during the 'second time' of the canter; at that particular moment the horse holds the leading front leg stretched out...above the ground, whilst his other three legs are all in support, on the ground. It is easy to ascertain that moment from the saddle...

Henry Wynmalen *Dressage A Study of the Finer Points of Riding*

**The academic Decarpentry employed the relatively new medium of cinema to study equine motion. This medium was especially useful in analysing complex movements such as the flying change. Here, he addresses this question of timing the aids.**

*Waldemar Seunig's line drawing of flying change from right to left, from* The Essence of Horsemanship.

Many riding masters have indicated precisely the moment when…the indication for the change of lead should be given to the horse. The moment indicated by each of them is not always the same. It is therefore appropriate to examine this problem.

To solve it completely, we would have to determine exactly the limits of time during which the change of lead, in front and behind, is possible, and outside of which it is *impossible*.

Decarpentry then states that:

The possibilities of animal mechanics are not well known enough to allow ourselves to be as categorical as this, and it is prudent to stick to the following probabilities...

Most significant of these are:

With the hind legs, which must change first, the reversal is difficult at the first time of canter, because the hind leg in support bears all the weight of the body and consequently is not very mobile...The facility of the change increases after the second time, when both hind legs are in suspension, and decreases again progressively as the hind legs come down...With the fore legs, the change is easy at the first time, as they are both off the ground, but it must be rejected because it causes disunitedness...

The change becomes difficult from the moment when the forehand starts coming down, i.e. at the second and third time, and afterwards becomes easy again up to the second time of the next cantering stride.

Therefore, to enable the horse to change lead easily it would appear to be sufficient that he should *want to do* so a short while before the third time, and during the phase of suspension. All riding masters are more or less in agreement on this point.

However, if he is to *want* to effectively, he must have first felt his rider's indication and had time to start executing it...

To achieve this result, the indication which must cause the beginning of the execution by the horse must first originate in the rider's brain and travel to the...aids, the sensations produced by them...on the horse's body must travel to his brain, and the latter must provoke the start of the mechanism...

Drawing on research by physiologists, Decarpentry reckoned that the average time taken for a thought to trigger a physical reaction was in the order of 1/10th second. However, each individual, whether human or equine, has an 'index of conductivity' – a personal reaction time – which may also be modified by practice and habit (as also suggested by Wynmalen). This latter point led Decarpentry to comment:

The moment indicated by the different masters as the one most favourable to provoke a beginning of execution…must be influenced…by the 'personal index of conductivity' of each of them, and also by that which they obtained from the average of the horses which they schooled…

We may also wonder whether they did not partly deceive themselves in indicating the precise moment when they thought they were giving the signal to the horse.

General Decarpentry  *Academic Equitation*

In other words, Decarpentry is speculating that some trainers may have been unaware of the inevitable time lapse between their instigation of the aid, and its physical implementation by the horse. Exploring this point further, he concludes that the aids for a flying change are better given relatively early in the stride sequence rather than relatively late – especially during the introductory stages – but that the horse's 'reaction time' is likely to speed up with practice, underscored with reward for a correct change.

## The Rider's Aids

Historically, there has been considerable debate about the aids for canter. If we consider that a particularly lively period of this debate occurred around the time that flying changes were being developed and absorbed into classical equitation, it will come as no surprise that this debate spilled over into this new field of discussion. In fact, if we consider that the essential mechanics of both canter and the flying change remain unchanged, it will be no surprise that elements of this debate continue to influence thinking.

Much of the original controversy centred on François Baucher, the acknowledged instigator of one-time changes. While Baucher's views on the precise nature of submission may have been highly personal, he makes what is essentially a salient point about preparation and balance:

To the mass of horsemen I address myself, when I say, either the horse is under the influence of your forces, and is entirely submissive to your power, or you are struggling with him...Changes of foot [lead] in such a state, can only be obtained by inclining the horse very much to one side, which makes the movement both difficult and ungraceful.

François Baucher *New Method of Horsemanship* in *François Baucher the Man and his Method by* Hilda Nelson

The studious General L'Hotte was, at one time, a pupil of Baucher's. Writing at the end of the nineteenth century, he brings the discussion of indirect and direct canter aids into the arena of flying changes.

If one were to ask for a lead change from a horse not yet familiar with this movement, one would have to force him into it by an inversion of the shoulders and the crossing of the haunches, which intelligent horsemen condemn.

What combination of aids must be used to obtain the intervention of the play of the lateral bipeds, which actually constitutes the lead change, there is no unanimity of opinion on the part of the *écuyers*. Agreement exists, however, on how the hand is used to lighten the shoulder which has to gain ground, which is, to bring back the weight of the forehand on to the shoulder which has to remain behind; that is, on to the right shoulder, if one goes from the right canter to the left canter. This can be achieved by opening the right rein if the neck is stiff; if it is supple, by flexing to the left and letting it flow back on to the left shoulder.

In Classical or *savante* equitation, perfection demands that weight displacement be reduced to the ultimate limits needed, by means of a light lateral effect of the hand and without modifying the direction of the neck; for any change in direction transmitted to this region, will affect the straight position of the horse in itself and the reaction it has on the haunches.

Where disagreement exists it is in the use of the heels [legs]. Some urge the use of the outside heels, also known as *opposing* heels; others the use of the inside heels, known as the *direct* heels. If these two methods are correctly used, both can give the sought for result. Thus for the horse cantering on the right leg, the lead change will be obtained by means of the opposing heel, that is, the right heel, when employed in such a way as to make the haunches deviate to the left; this deviation pushes the left hock forward while making the horse traverse, which he does naturally when he canters on the left leg. [**This statement seems to indicate that L'Hotte accepted that most horses – at least before their schooling is complete – are naturally crooked in left canter**]. The same lead change is obtained by means of the direct heel, that is, the left heel, when it is used...in such a way as to draw the left hock under the centre of the mass.

These two methods find their use:

The first one, when the horse's obedience to the aid is not complete. On the other hand, it satisfies all the requirements dealing with cross-country equitation. Furthermore, the horse can, without any inconvenience, traverse a little in the practice of ordinary equitation.

The second one, a more refined and delicate use, offers…the advantage of keeping the horse straight, an invaluable advantage for this type of equitation, enabling one, without difficulty, to obtain lead changes at every three strides, two strides, and at every stride 'a tempo'.

This is understandable. The straight horse avoids any traversing and inflexions on the side…

Alexis-François L'Hotte  *Questions Équestres* (in *Alexis-François L'Hotte The Quest For Lightness In Equitation*, by Hilda Nelson)

**Geoffrey Brooke, who was Chief Instructor to the British Cavalry School in the 1920s, shares L'Hotte's aim of achieving straightness. He proposes the initial use of diagonal aids to produce the change, these being modified and lightened progressively. (His final aids are very similar to those described by Wynmalen for the basic transition into canter.)**

We will assume that he is cantering with the off-fore leading… First warning can be given by a gentle feeling of the left rein, followed by a slightly stronger pressure of the right leg. The horse's instant reactions are [to] the warning touch of the left rein reinforced by pressure of the right leg indicating primary impulsion from the off-hind leg, which will start the new cycle of movement with the near-fore leading…Soon the slightest warning touch of the rein should suffice so that there should be no constriction on the horse's head play [natural cyclic movement of the head] associated with canter.

In the same way we will reach the stage when leg pressure need not be applied behind the girth and consequently there will be no indication or inclination on the part of the horse to deflect from a straight line. Experienced riders knowing the reactions of a well-trained horse will be equally aware of their own sensations and the delicacy required in the execution of this aid. The novice, once he understands the reason for his actions and their effect on his mount, will by patience and perseverance himself attain the same standard when, with imperceptible aids, his horse makes a perfectly smooth change on a straight line.

Geoffrey Brooke  *Horsemanship Dressage & Show-Jumping*

*Change of lead from near fore to off fore: Mrs V.D.S. Williams on Pilgrim, from Geoffrey Brooke's* Horsemanship, Dressage and Show-Jumping.

John Winnett's reasoning runs along similar lines. He begins with the premise that...

...the flying change can be considered as a new canter depart, and the aids for the flying changes are the same as for the canter depart; outside leg behind the girth to suggest, inside leg at the girth to demand...

However, he agrees with L'Hotte that predominant use of the direct (inside) aids helps to promote straightness, and stresses the need for subtlety:

The aids must remain quiet and subtle...I put more emphasis on my inside leg, for I have found that I can make my changes straighter with more forward thrust from the horse's new inside hind. Swinging the outside leg back and forth on the horse's flanks can only disrupt the horse's balance and straightness...The rider's seat must remain vertical and supple in the saddle...The upper body must never swing from side to side.

John Winnett *Dressage as Art in Competition*

Winnett's strictures regarding excessively strong aids are echoed widely:

The changes should be asked for calmly and there should be no visible or audible effort on the rider's part as he asks for them... Remember that it is of primary importance to have the form of the canter correct before any changes are asked for, and increasing the intensity of the aids will not help unless the canter is good.

Nuno Oliveira *Notes and Reminiscences of a Portuguese Rider*

Greif taught me that the rider should not attempt to indicate this change of lead by twisting his body or throwing it from one side to the other but by quietly changing the aids of legs and reins...

Alois Podhajsky *My Horses, My Teachers*

In conclusion, we may add that any unnecessary tossing about of the rider's body...merely dulls the horse's responses to the rein and leg controls instead of making it easier for the horse to change the lead...An artist achieves his greatest effects by using the maximum economy of gesture.

Waldemar Seunig *Horsemanship*

I have seen the faces of old master trainers as they watched riders who swung all over in the saddle and pushed the horse's hindquarters one way and the other. Theirs is not a look you want aimed in your direction as a rider.

Paul Belasik *Dressage for the 21st Century*

**Seunig and Belasik are two authorities who highlight the subtle involvement of the rider's seat in effecting the flying change.**

During suspension, that is, at the instant of the change of lead, the small of the rider's back and his legs...drive the horse straight ahead, using pressure that is more or less pronounced. The rider's hand allows the new inner side to go forward, while the new outside seat bone exerts greater load in order to facilitate an earlier grounding of the hind leg, which was formerly the inside one.

Waldemar Seunig *Horsemanship*

**Belasik examines the role of the seat in some depth, prescribing unequivocally his view that it is the seat aids, rather than strong leg aids, that should predominate in the flying change:**

Before discussing the 'where' of the flying change, the 'how' should be clarified. Flying changes seem to be taught around the world in two distinct schools. In one, the change is initiated and controlled by strong leg aids, which predominate over the seat. In the other, the change is initiated by seat and weight aids, which predominate over the legs.

The main problem with changing with the lower legs is that, by now, the horse has been taught leg-yielding, shoulder-in, travers, renvers, half-pass, and even counter-changes of hand. If the lower legs are used, particularly if one is used more strongly and further back than the other, it will be virtually impossible to make straight changes, which are a premier requirement of classic changes. The horse will do exactly what it has been trained to do – swing the haunches away from the leg…When riders learn this method, or begin training this way, a whole system of defensive maneuvers ensues. They know the change is supposed to be straight but they can't stop the swing with their legs. They try to block the horse with the reins, usually grabbing the outside rein in an effort to prevent the drift. This blocks impulsion, so the rider's body gets thrown more into the movement in an attempt to produce more forward momentum. When the haunches swing out and the rider tries to change back, horse and rider are so far out of line that the horse's neck is bent back in the opposite direction. Eventually the warp is amplified. When the rider changes off the lower leg or spur, the hip and seat move. However, when they follow the leg in this way, it is almost as a ricochet or recoil. The change is late and the rider often bumps the horse in the back at the critical time of the change over, making even semi-successful clean changes hollow. I do not know why this system is still evident…but it is.

Classical, straight changes are initiated with the back, seat and hips. The hips of the rider become one with the hips of the horse. In informal practice, if one were to watch the riders who change this way, the rider's lower legs may swing. This would lead one to believe that the rider is signaling the change with the lower leg. However, if one were to look very carefully, say with a slow motion video camera…one would see that the lower leg is, in fact, often too late to make the change, which has already taken place. In fact, the subtle but clear actions of the hips, upper leg, thigh and back, has made the change and the lower leg is following the inertia created by the seat…The seat predominates: everything is in perfect timing. When changes are trained and executed in this way, the horse will remain straight. The hips of both horse and rider will change like those of a cross-country skier. The legs track in two straight lines like skis. The left hip and leg advance, then the right, then the left, etc. When the hips create the change, the seat will be pushing the change. The changes will be light and round, and when it comes to the multiple changes these will hold a straight line. In this system, the rider will never be behind the motion, grinding the horse's back down into a hollow pose, thus making the hind legs change late.                    Paul Belasik *Dressage for the 21st Century*

**Henry Wynmalen also makes the point that inappropriate actions by the rider may easily hinder the horse. His emphasis is on avoiding over-restriction with the reins.**

The change of leg in the air, or flying change…is a perfectly natural movement to the horse; it causes him no difficulty.

Yet it is far from easy to obtain a correct change of leg on demand. But the cause of that difficulty lies entirely with the rider and not with the horse. It is not easy to apply the aids which are required without hindering his execution of this delicate movement…

Now let us examine the rider's difficulties. They lie in the application of the aids…

The aids [to canter] have been described…it has been stressed that any resistance by the bit to forward movement will mar the strike-off…it can now be added that any resistance by the bit during the moment of the change will ruin the change…In the strike-off, the difficulty is caused by the momentary acceleration. In the change there is no acceleration. But, in changing, the horse lengthens momentarily; head and neck stretch forward somewhat and dip to some extent from side to side. Hence, though the causes of the difficulty…are not identical, the need to avoid rein interference is the same…

To succeed with the changes, the horse must be collected… but in the natural form of the canter and not pulled together; if

*Change of lead to near fore: Henry Wynmalen on Bascar.*

the rein be too short, the neck has insufficient freedom and the horse will be hindered in the liberty of his stride; if the stride be too short, the execution of the change will become very difficult. It will be appreciated that these hindrances, all, are of the rider's making.

Lastly…deceleration…is fatal. It will rob the horse of the possibility to complete a pure change…

Henry Wynmalen   *Dressage A Study of the Finer Points of Riding*

**Wynmalen's views on this issue are very much in accord with those of Richard Wätjen…**

Furthermore, it is of vital importance to give the horse enough freedom at the very moment of the change, so that from the very beginning it learns to execute the change *with impulsion* and in a *straight forward* direction.        Richard Wätjen   *Dressage Riding*

…and General Decarpentry:

For the change of lead…to be correct, i.e. *executed* in front and behind during the same stride, the *hind pair* must always change first. If the fore legs change first, then the next stride will always be *disunited*…

…To allow the horse to change behind first without difficulty …his quarters must be very free, and therefore considerably unloaded. Consequently, in the first attempts at obtaining a change, the horse must be allowed to lower his forehand, his neck should not be shortened much, and the angle of the poll should be a little open rather than too closed…

The canter should be neither too slow, nor too collected. A longer and lengthier period of suspension greatly increase the ease with which the inversion of the limbs can be made.

General Decarpentry   *Academic Equitation*

In a similar vein, Alfred Knopfhart warns that any extreme actions or practices by the rider will interfere with the execution of the change:

…The right degree of collection varies with the individual but, in any case, active elevation of head and neck, which stiffens the back, or over-bending (a fault often due to the use of draw reins), which causes overloading of the forehand, equally impairs the fluency of the change.

Alfred Knopfhart  *Dressage A Guidebook for the Road to Success*

Reiterating Wynmalen's view, that a fluent flying change is relatively easy for an unencumbered horse, Kurt Albrecht makes the point that, ultimately, it is the rider who must learn precision. (The message of the final sentence may well transcend the specifics of the flying change.)

Although horses will change legs fluently when they gallop at pasture, they usually find changes difficult when they have to carry a rider at canter…This goes to show – since the movement is such a natural one for the horse – that it is not easy for the rider to learn to move in perfect unison with the horse at the rhythm of canter. At the stage of teaching the horse to understand the requirement, it needs only a minute delay in giving the aids or the smallest discord of aids to make the change difficult or impossible for the horse. Later, when he has learnt to understand the message, the slightest indication will be sufficient to get him to execute the movement, and he may even perform a correct change despite inadequate aids.

Kurt Albrecht  *Principles of Dressage*

## *Introducing the Single Change*

The more deliberately and methodically we proceed in this first lesson, the more rapid progress will be. We should arrange matters so that the exercises in the flying changes...are scheduled at the end of the...lesson; we dismount as soon as the successful change is made and lead the horse back to the stable.

Waldemar Seunig *Horsemanship*

It is likely that these words of Seunig's would meet with virtually universal approval from the Masters. The concepts of methodical deliberation, and of not being over-demanding, are widely echoed. It is, however, a fact that different individuals have their preferred method (or methods) of approaching this exercise. Furthermore, many authorities agree that it may be appropriate to tailor the approach according to the characteristics of the individual horse. It may be, therefore, that the wise trainer will build up a 'library' of methods from which valuable ideas can be extracted.

Seunig, himself, readily acknowledges the diversity of approaches:

There are many 'recipes' for making it easier to exercise the flying change...One rider swears by change of lead at the crossing of a figure of eight, while the other follows Fillis and makes the change in the corner...

We who are in no hurry to exercise the flying change and begin it only when the horse lets us know that it is ready for it think that the straight road is the safest and best...At the beginning changing the lead along a straight line is easier for the horse than changing it on a half-circle, because on the latter the moment the rider changes seat must coincide exactly with the instant the horse enters upon the new turn. Besides, this figure requires a greater shift of seat. The rider's change of seat must always occur in such a way that it is unnoticeable to a spectator.

Waldemar Seunig  *Horsemanship*

**Elsewhere in the same work, Seunig makes points about avoiding anticipation on the horse's part…**

At the outset it is well to execute the change several times at the same point on each hand. But once the horse has acquired some degree of assurance, the same line must be ridden across the ring without a change to keep the horse from anticipating the rider's controls and making a change automatically.

Waldemar Seunig  *Horsemanship*

**Fillis's method, as mentioned by Seunig, is described in *Breaking and Riding* thus:**

To obtain a change of leg, I proceed in the following manner: I start the horse into the canter with the off fore while going to the right. When he has gone some strides on this leg, I stop him and make him start off on the near fore while circling to the right, and taking care to hold him as straight as possible. I repeat this work several times, and continue it until I feel that the horse is perfectly light in hand, and that he will start off into the canter at the slightest pressure of the legs, without hurrying himself and without trying to carry his haunches out of the straight line…

I…start him into the canter on the off fore, and keep him at it until he becomes quiet. I then walk him for a minute or two, and put him into canter on the near fore, and keep him at it…until he is light and quiet, after which I again walk him for some moments. Finally, I start him into canter on the off fore, and so on. I therefore make successive starts at the canter, each one being on a different leg. Little by little I shorten the periods during which I let the horse walk between the starts…At last he learns to start into the canter alternately from the stationary foot to the other foot, the starts being interrupted only by the halt…

At this period of his training the horse is ready for the change of leg, which I ought to be able to make him do without upsetting him in the least. I start him into the canter on the near fore, while going to the right. He therefore canters on the outward leg, and I support him …with the near rein and right leg, which gives a stronger pressure than the left leg. When I come to a corner of the school I completely change my 'aids' and use the off rein and left leg. This change of 'aids' ought to be done with great decision and perfect combination…This quickness and smoothness are possible only if the rider has constantly taken the precaution of lightly feeling the off rein, and of keeping the left leg very close to the animal's side, so that he need only feel this rein a little stronger and press the leg a little more. As the horse has already lightly felt the off rein, and as the left leg has been kept very close to his side, there will be neither jerk nor irritation…when this hand and leg predominate in their turn.

Finally, as we have practised our horse to start on the off leg …and as we ask him to do this first change of leg when turning to the right, which will be easier for him to do…he will rarely refuse to obey, even at the first time.

If, however, he does not obey, we must not persist in roughly forcing him, because that would…make him afraid of the change of leg, which he would not understand. He should be stopped, brought into hand at the walk, made to start on the near fore, and then asked to change his leg. But before doing this we should wait until he is quiet.

The fact of the horse failing to do a change of leg several times, is proof that his preparation is insufficient; that being surprised by the 'aids' he tried to escape or throw himself to one side; or that he did not understand what we wanted...Whenever we meet with a difficulty, we should go back to the start...

James Fillis *Breaking and Riding*

While Fillis makes the initial change from counter-canter in a corner, Decarpentry makes it on a circle. However, there is a marked similarity between their methods, and both entail a good deal of preparation in transitions between canter and walk. Decarpentry had strong views about this preparatory work...

The horse must strike off from the walk to the canter on either lead, in a perfectly straight position, at the same even rhythm, and with the same amplitude of movement.

From the canter on either lead, he must come back to a perfectly regular walk with the same promptness and the same ease...

...his even stronger views, proscribing transitions between canter and trot, may give historical insight as to the type of horse with which he was familiar, especially in the earlier part of his career:

The transition to the canter *from the trot*, and especially from the canter *to the trot* must be absolutely avoided during the whole period of the education to the changes, and this applies to all horses but especially those which have even a distant trotting ancestry. These have a marked disposition to insert a trotting stride in passing from one canter to the other...once the horse has been allowed to perform the change in this manner, the fault often becomes ineradicable; it robs the changes of all value and eventually makes the changes at every stride *impossible.*]

General Decarpentry  *Academic Equitation*

**Regarding 'The Lesson of the Change', Decarpentry says:**

The horse must be perfectly relaxed and calm. In the preparatory work, the rider will only demand exercises and movements which the horse executes willingly, and will reward him with special generosity if they have been performed well.

**[From an active, *slightly* shortened walk on a circle right]**

He will then get the horse to strike off at the canter *on the right lead, always at the same part* of the circle [**Decarpentry recommends A or C**]…Each strike off should be followed by only a few strides at the canter, with a return to the walk after approximately a half-circle. Every time the rider asks the horse to strike off, he uses the customary aids, and accompanies them by the indication of the voice…This work is persevered with, until the horse strikes off almost automatically on the command of the voice, the other aids being almost unnecessary.

Once this first 'convention' is well understood by rider and horse, the latter is again allowed to do one or two circles [circuits] of the manège at a relaxed walk [**author's footnote: still on the right rein**], then is put on the bit again, and cantered *on the left lead* [i.e. in **counter-canter**] after he has gone *well past* the centre of the narrow side of the school…When the rider reaches the centre of the short side [**where he had previously asked for canter right from walk**] he *quietly* gives his indications for the canter right, accompanied by the aid of the voice, and waits while renewing his indications *without at any moment increasing their intensity.*

Usually the horse instantly manifests a quickening of his

attention – and his perplexity – and *attempts* 'something', but with some hesitation. He attempts to change the gait and its regularity is lost; he may put in a number of false beats…and after a certain time, maybe rather a long one…succeed in changing to the right lead. The rider should *immediately* and lengthily caress the horse, allow him to canter for a circuit or two, come back to the walk, and give a long period of rest.

If the horse does not react to the demand for canter on the right lead…or…stops reacting before having achieved the change of lead – and this is rare – the rider should quietly come back to the walk and ask for canter right by the means used previously…and start again.

We should only resort to this procedure if the horse does not react to some extent or at all. For so long as he manifestly shows that he is trying to obey his rider's indications he must be allowed to go on attempting to do so…

If the first change of lead has been obtained without too much difficulty, as is usually the case…two or three consecutive demands can be made during this first lesson, each one separated from the other by a long period of rest…so the horse can be confirmed in his understanding…while no unfair advantage is taken of his co-operativeness.

If, on the contrary, this first change has presented prolonged difficulty, the rider should remain content with only one transition from canter to canter, then immediately dismount and lead the horse back to the stable.

General Decarpentry Academic Equitation

**Henry Wynmalen advocated asking for initial changes at the end of a diagonal:**

Now to execute the first change I will canter my horse round the school to the right and do a diagonal change of hands; going along the diagonal I will...apply the aids for the right canter more markedly, collect him carefully and...hold him very straight. On arriving at the far end of the diagonal the horse will have to change, since he will have to turn to the left.

At the precise moment of entering the turn I reverse my aids...and in every case my horse will change at the first time of asking, because his preparation has been right.

Henry Wynmalen *Equitation*

In Dressage *A Study of the Finer Points of Riding*, Wynmalen says of the moment of the change:

We do not swing the horse; that is quite unnecessary...and leads to disunited changes. We simply reverse the aids. We realize that each change is in essence no other than a new start at the canter with the other leg leading. We do one change only, and walk for a while. If we fail, we also walk for a while before we try again.

After advising patience in establishing the initial changes...

We are quite satisfied...with but a few successful changes every day. We avoid asking the change in the same place; in so doing, we avoid routine.

As the days wear on we ask for more changes, but never very many...and we keep up the practice of walking for a while after each change...for the sake of calmness, which is absolutely essential for this work.

...Wynmalen proceeds to changes on a straight line. Typically for him, he prefers to do this work in the open:

When the changes done with the help of a change of direction have become established, are smooth, easy and fluent, we will ask for a change on a straight line. I prefer to do this work in the open, away from the school. In that way the horse can canter on long straight lines and there is nothing to encourage anticipations. We canter along quietly, bring the horse on the aids, do our change and walk…It is only when I am really satisfied that the horse does his one change perfectly…that I keep him cantering…and ask for two, perhaps three changes at intervals of perhaps twenty or thirty strides.

The whole basis of this work is purity of change, on demand, calm. The entire further progress is built up on just that. We will not succeed if we attempt to hurry progress and repeat the same exercise too often or for too long a time…

Henry Wynmalen  *Dressage A Study of the Finer Points of Riding*

**John Winnett's preparatory work has a good deal in common with that of Fillis and Decarpentry except that, in the early stages, he is prepared to ride transitions between canter and trot. However, he shares Decarpentry's view that the canter aid should tend towards being an interior lateral aid. While his siting of the early changes takes account of the individual horse, he does not execute changes on circles.**

Flying changes must never be trained by rupture of balance, throwing the horse from side to side. The basic training must start…in transitions trot, canter, trot; walk, canter, walk, and then build up to simple changes at X, and along the wall of the riding hall. At this stage, very careful attention must be paid to the canter depart. To canter on, I *suggest* with my outside leg and *demand* the transition with my inside leg at the girth. Within a short period, the horse will strike off to my inside leg only. I use my hands as little as possible…The canter departs can be made out of shoulder-fore initially to ensure that the inside hind leg does not swing or deviate to the inside. If the eventual flying changes are to be dead straight, then the canter departs must be straight and flawless from the beginning…

…I start to ask for successive simple changes – walk eight strides, canter eight strides, alternating leads left, right; right, left. When the eights are established, calm, forward and straight, I move on to sequences of five, four, three and eventually two strides. During this stage of training I also ask for canter departs out of the full halt, and rein-backs; again alternating leads.

Once these simple changes have been perfected, I ask for one flying change. If I am working with a highly spirited horse, I usually choose to ask for the first change at the end of a half circle of 10 metres, or on the short diagonal where I can use the wall to restrain the forward jump instead of having to use a strong half-halt, which would restrict the new inside hind leg from swinging through to its fullest engagement. On the other hand, if I have a lazy horse, I will ask for the change at the end of the long diagonal, or before the entrance of a corner where I have a long straight line to establish more impulsion. I never ask for changes on a circle, since one cannot execute a straight change on a curved line. Flying changes performed on a circle serve as a guise for bad flying changes.

John Winnett  *Dressage as Art in Competition*

André Jousseaume's approach shows some similarity to Winnett's in initial siting, and to Wynmalen's in terms of preparatory aids.

The first changes of lead will be demanded at the end of a half-circle or at the end of a diagonal. To simplify this work, the rider's demands must be made at the precise instant when the horse returns to the track.

When at canter on the right lead:

1. Change the bend and left bearing rein to straighten the horse and put him in the position favourable to the canter to the left.
2. Reverse the leg action, and, as in the beginning of the demands for canter departs, be sure to have clear and precise aids without forgetting the change of seat.
3. At the same time, action of the left hand, same action as for canter departs, that is, successive tightening of the fingers with successive elevations of the hand, tightening and elevations effected simultaneously. Wait for the change of lead to happen.

...As with any movement, begin with the side which seems easier...canter on the lead which the horse likes less; since he prefers...the other lead, he will be all the more willing to change. Later, the other lead will be given special attention.

Jousseaume also prescribes a set progression of exercises:

The steps to follow are:

1. Change of lead at the end of the half-circle or the diagonal.
2. Change of lead on the circle from the counter canter.
3. Change of lead on the straight line.
4. Change of lead on the circle from the true canter.

André Jousseaume *Progressive Dressage*

While this specific progression might not find universal favour, a number of authorities subscribe to broadly similar notions.

Jousseaume's fourth point, regarding changes to counter-canter on a circle, highlights what is, at least, a point of interest – in fact Decarpentry, in *Academic Equitation*, goes on to mention changes 'a tempo' on circles, an exercise that would doubtless give rise to great debate.

Like Winnett, Podhajsky believes in choosing an approach which suits the individual horse, although he is prepared to continue the exercise of changing through trot or walk until it becomes a flying change through a figure of eight.

When ready to try flying changes, the rider must consider the conformation of his horse and proceed in the way easiest for him. A good method is to change through the diagonal…and apply the aids for changing the leg a little more emphatically at the moment the horse passes through the first corner. The aids are exactly the same as for the strike-off on the other leg and must be done without reducing the canter to a lower speed…The rider must avoid twisting his body in all directions, which is so often the case.

Another method of teaching the flying change is to do it at the point where the rein is changed when changing the circle. When this transition can be made without difficulty through a short and supple change at the trot and walk, the flying change can be asked by applying the same aids as described above. If the flying change has been correctly made, the horse should be immediately rewarded by a walk on the loose rein. If the change was not correct, the rider must go back to the preparation…On no account must the horse be punished.

Alois Podhajsky    *The Complete Training of Horse and Rider*

**Like Jousseaume, Podhajsky has his own preferred progression:**

When the flying change can be correctly performed in the corner of the school or when changing the circle, it may be practised on a straight line, first in the middle of the diagonal when changing rein, then after a turn and change of rein, and at last alongside the wall. It is more important in all these exercises that the hind legs spring smoothly under the body. The smooth rhythm of the movement must not be interrupted and the change must be absolutely straight and forward.

Alois Podhajsky  *The Complete Training of Horse and Rider*

Paul Belasik is prepared to use both the figure of eight (via simple changes through trot) and transitions from counter-canter. *In Riding Towards the Light*, he writes:

There are two main methods that I use to teach the flying change. Each has its good points and I use whichever seems to fit the horse better. One way is to circle the horse at canter. As I complete the circle, I make a downward transition to trot. I change the bend to the opposite direction, strike off on the opposite lead and circle in that direction. When I come back to the middle, I go back to trot, change direction and go off again on the opposite lead. As the horse becomes more proficient, I reduce the number of trot strides until, when I feel the horse is ready, I skip the trot entirely, asking with firm aids to change leads from canter to canter...

Under the other system, I canter down the long side of the...arena, and about half way down, I start a small circle. Instead of completing it, halfway around I head back to the wall on a small diagonal. When I return to the wall I will be counter-cantering and about to ride through the corner of the arena. Just as I approach the corner of the arena I ask for a change. Often the horse obliges because it prefers to return to the true canter. Also, the relief from the extra stretch of the counter-canter is welcome. This method has the benefit of being next to a wall when changing, which helps to keep the horse straighter.

Paul Belasik  *Riding Towards the Light*

In *Dressage for the 21st Century*, Belasik also describes essentially the same method as Fillis of changing from counter-canter in a corner:

One of the most common approaches is to go down the long wall in the counter-canter. On the corner, the rider collects the horse more than usual. The rider would almost want the horse to feel suspicious – this will not feel the same as continuing through the corner in the counter-canter. When the horse and rider are just about to enter the corner, the rider asks for the change. If it fails, the rider must wait a few strides to see if the horse will get the idea and make the change. If it does not, the rider makes a transition to the trot, or walk, and does a simple change. The rider must show the horse what is required.

**He also summarises the advantages and disadvantages of changing both from counter-canter and on the figure of eight:**

The advantage of training the change from the counter-canter to the true canter is that it is the horse's natural inclination to get out of the counter-canter to the true canter. Also, and very important, there is the fact that the wall will serve as a straight line to help keep the horse from huge sideways deviations, even when changing toward the arena. The disadvantage is that, with some horses, this method will ruin the reliability of the counter-canter for a while. A few horses will feel trapped by the wall and perform better in free space.

The advantages of training on the figure of eight are twofold. First, that a very clear change of direction and rein from one true canter to the other is present. Second, since the counter-canter has been left out of the exercise, it eliminates confusion if the horse starts to anticipate the change. The disadvantage is that the horse and rider are out in the open and, if the horse becomes crooked, the change can become crooked. It is much more difficult to keep the horse straight in a free space with no wall.

Belasik also makes an observation that has bearing on preparing the horse to change, and also avoiding anticipation on the horse's part.

From the beginning, the rider must tell the horse, 'I will never initiate a flying change without a set up, a little collection, and a little surge of power'. Then, if the rider approaches a turn in the counter-canter with seat relaxed and back swinging, the horse will stay in the counter-canter. If, however, the rider braces the back and collects the horse, the horse is being prepared to change. The rider is telling the horse 'I may change my seat and hips, and you must follow'.

Paul Belasik  *Dressage for the 21st Century*

On the subject of anticipation, Alfred Knopfhart, writing primarily of counter-canter, makes a wry observation:

During the…period of schooling necessary to teach the horse to counter-canter, he may…change lead in mid-air in a turn rather than experience the difficulty of counter-cantering through a corner. In fact, the flying change unintended by the rider is frequently much more fluent than the ones which he subsequently tries to obtain in obedience to the conventional aids! This may show that the horse has a favorable aptitude for the change…but it also shows that he changes perfectly fluently only when the decision to do so is his own…

He goes on to add:

A perceptive rider will either drive the horse firmly forwards in counter-canter when he feels it is about to change, or better still, will change his own position to accord with the change and ride the horse on calmly in the new canter. He must on no account punish the horse for doing something which he will eventually be asked to do.

Alfred Knopfhart  *Dressage A Guidebook for the Road to Success*

It is one of the qualities of the Masters that they do not deny the existence of problems and difficulties. Instead, they analyse them and look for the best means of resolving them. Nuno Oliveira states plainly that...

...there are exceptionally reticent horses who have great difficulty in flying changes, and then only the great masters who have enormous experience and virtuosity, can succeed in resolving this problem.  Nuno Oliveira  *Reflections on Equestrian Art*

While Knopfhart writes:

...one recognizes genuine experts by their awareness and admission of their own difficulties. They appreciate the knowledge and the advice of their fellows. It is only the dilettante who boasts that he never has any problems and does not need help; he may not know it but it is unlikely that he will get very far.

Alfred Knopfhart  *Dressage A Guidebook for the Road to Success*

In the same book, Knopfhart discusses some of the difficulties that may confront even the most astute of trainers during the introduction of the flying change.

One will always have to take into account the mental as well as the physical aptitudes of the horse for the flying change...There are no aids which can force the horse to change legs in the air. The animal must have the right instinct for it and a cheerful disposition...Natural bodily adroitness, and pure enjoyment of movement are essential ingredients in the recipe for the flying change...

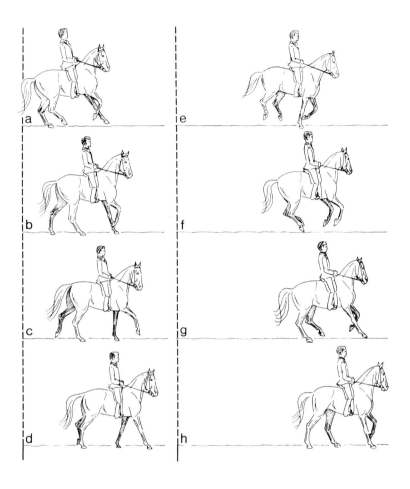

*Flying change from right to left.* **a-e** = *Right canter;* **e, f** = *Change of position;* **f** = *Change of lead at the moment of suspension;* **g, h** = *Left canter.*

*Flying change from right to left, from Alfred Knopfhart's*
Dressage A Guidebook for the Road to Success.

Yet, however well-prepared a horse may be, one can expect a certain difficulty, unprecedented in previous canter lessons when teaching him to execute perfect flying changes. There are many well-known methods and a few not-well-known ones of over-coming the difficulty, any one of which may be appropriate to a particular case. Finding the right one is a matter of experience, feeling and, to some extent, of intuition. There is no standard recipe because every horse is an individual…

While the teaching of simple changes is based on an under-standing of the mechanics of the horse, the teaching of flying changes is more a matter of artistic ability. It requires at least as much understanding as technical competence. By sticking stub-bornly to a method which is unsuitable for a particular animal, one faces frustrating difficulty or even complete failure…

One should not hesitate to abandon one method as soon as it seems that it is not leading to success. Dogged adhesion to one system shows poor horsemanship…nevertheless, the basic principles of dressage need to be understood and respected – adaptability does not mean haphazard experimentation.

Whichever system one starts with, fine feeling and acute observation of the horse's reaction are essential; even so it is not easy to judge events accurately from the saddle. One cannot really dispense with the assistance of an expert who can see horse and rider as a whole and is able to give advice…

**Of all early attempts to achieve a flying change, the author says:**

The outcome will vary depending on the idiosyncratic canter action and sensitivity of the horse. With horses that are inclined to rush or pull, it is unwise to let them gain speed and the point of change must be chosen with discernment (the best place is probably just before approaching a corner of the arena). On the contrary, with horses that tend to lag, one usually has to drive forward more emphatically.

Alfred Knopfhart  *Dressage A Guidebook for the Road to Success*

**André Jousseaume warns against impatient over-reaction to lack of understanding or nervousness on the horse's part:**

It is evident that, as long as the reflexes are not educated, there will be hesitation on the part of the horse, which will not immediately understand this new demand…Most of the time, it will only be after several successive demands…that he will decide to carry out the change of lead, but, if the rider rewards instantly, this hesitation will quickly disappear…

If, in spite of a correct demand, the horse does not obey… bring him back to a state of calm because he will inevitably be nervous…if the horse is too nervous, it is better to stop the lesson and take it up again later. Nervousness does not come from unwillingness, but from lack of understanding. Afterwards, ask only for a few changes of lead at a time. There is always a tendency to demand too much. Progress will be felt not by the number of changes…performed, but by seeking a progressively more correct way of doing them.

André Jousseaume  *Progressive Dressage*

**In a similar vein, Seunig stresses the need for calmness in both horse and rider…**

The change should never be executed if the horse manifests any uneasiness during preparatory collection. Calmly continuing to gallop as if nothing had happened is the best remedy for rushing, fearful pushing to the side and anticipating. But if we are surprised by a premature change or by the horse crossing its legs, we deliberately pass to the walk and resume the *original* schooled gallop (not a gallop offered spontaneously by the horse) only after the horse has calmed down completely. We should attempt another flying change from this gallop only after the horse remains calm after repeated simple changes...

...and, again, advises patience:

Some riders torment themselves and their horses with uninterrupted 'exercising' of the flying changes and still fail to achieve absolute certainty...These are the riders who were unable to display enough patience and understanding during the preceding work...They began flying changes before their horse was able to take gallop departs straight on either lead and before it had achieved the necessary certainty and responsiveness in the simple changes on a straight, free track. That is why we must not grow obstinate about difficulties that may arise in exercising the flying change and try to compel a change of lead. We reduce our demands for the time being. The fruit is not yet ripe.

Waldemar Seunig  *Horsemanship*

His views being echoed by Richard Wätjen:

If a horse does not respond to the first indication, one should not force the change, but one should start again after the horse has been properly prepared. If a horse is *especially* difficult to change, then the fault lies in the fact that the horse has not yet *reached the proper stage of training...*  Richard Wätjen  *Dressage Riding*

Paul Belasik focuses on the aptitude of the individual horse:

In all fairness to the trainers who did not feel that the changes were a true classical exercise, one that is developed and improves with strength and practice, no other movement seems to be such a matter of genetics. Horses born with the ability to change can do so correctly from the first day they are introduced to the movement. Other horses have no inclination to change and training them to do the flying changes can be a long and arduous process.

I have had horses in training that executed three clean flying changes on crossing the centerline of a three-loop serpentine on the first day I asked for them. I have also had horses that have taken a year to achieve the same pattern consistently. It seems to have little to do with a conscientious preparatory training program, although control in the multiple changes definitely does.

Paul Belasik *Dressage for the 21st Century*

On the same theme, Knopfhart expands upon the possible reasons for difficulty, and emphasises that patient persistence may eventually provide the key:

If all one's efforts remain unavailing, it may be that the horse has absolutely no aptitude for flying changes (which can only be decided after repeated attempts at intervals of some months) or that he is not ready for the lesson. This can be a question of age, of intelligence, or of deficient tractability. Horse do not all reach maturity at the same age. With sufficiently long experience of training horses...one will have met with some that despite excellent aptitudes, competent and carefully progressive training, have defeated so many endeavors to get them to execute a correct flying change as to make one seriously start to doubt their suitability for competition at a high level of proficiency. But after a long, though 'creative pause', all of a sudden they take to the exercise with every appearance of enjoyment...Time can work wonders. It may seem that to have to wait three years before a horse is ready to compete at Third Level is excessive, but one should reflect that most have needed a much longer period of preparation. And after achieving the first correct isolated flying change, the series of changes...are still very far away.

Alfred Knopfhart  *Dressage A Guidebook for the Road to Success*

## *Faults in the Change*

Two Masters give us brief descriptions of the qualities that characterise correct changes:

The flying change of lead must take place smoothly while advancing, without hesitation and on a single track.

Waldemar Seunig  *Horsemanship*

The characteristics of a good change are: lightness, precision, straight horse, and amplitude of movement.

André Jousseaume  *Progressive Dressage*

It will therefore be apparent that faulty changes are those that are lacking in these qualities.

Having provided a warning against impatience, which he sees as the root cause of many faults, Podhajsky lists a number of common ones:

A temptation that must be guarded against, especially by young riders, is that, overcome by the joy of having obtained the change, they practise it too often, forgetting the fatigue caused to the horse. This is the origin of many faults. In the same way faults will be caused by starting the exercise before the horse has acquired sufficient strength. The horse will change in front before he changes behind or vice versa, or the change will not be made with a full stride, especially of the hind legs. These faults will be difficult to eliminate, as horses often acquire great skill in performing them and even deceive their riders...

Many other faults may appear, such as deviation of the quarters to the side on which the horse is crooked; swinging the quarters on both sides at the moment of change, because the horse has been allowed to strike off into the canter by bringing the hindquarters in; changing with the hindquarters too high because the joints of the hind legs are not sufficiently bent; changes without gaining ground to the front...Some horses get upset and try to rush away when the change is asked, because they have been forced to do it before they are ready...The great variety of faults that can be made is a distinct proof of the high degree of proficiency and suppleness required before the rider may demand this difficult exercise...

Alois Podhajsky  *The Complete Training of Horse and Rider*

Perhaps the most fundamental fault is the disunited change. Fillis lays the blame for 'unscheduled' disunited changes squarely at the feet of the rider:

The pitfall in the changes of leg exist entirely in the preparations which the breaker [rider] generally makes to obtain them. Of course, I do not allude to the preparation of the horse...but only to the movements of the breaker before the exact moment when he wants the horse to change. It is extremely important that he remains quiet while the horse is taking his strides, during which the animal should not change...If he touches the reins, the forehand will change, and if he alters the position of his legs, the hind quarters will change. But as there will be no harmony between the 'aids', the horse will not change legs.

It is wrong to blame the horse for becoming disunited, because in such cases the rider almost always provokes him to do so...

James Fillis  *Breaking and Riding*

Whilst agreeing that the rider may well be at fault, Knopfhart also points to possible inadequacies in the horse's training. (Since these, too, could be ultimately blamed upon the way the horse has been ridden, it may be that he is alluding to the remedy of faults inherited from elsewhere).

If the horse changes behind before changing in front or conversely, the rider or the horse can be at fault. In the first instance, either the half halt or the aids for change may be inadequate.

But it is not always the rider's fault. It can be that of the horse, for any number of reasons...For example, a basically faulty canter, with even only slightly delayed or hurried footfalls behind, nearly always produces an impure canter change. In this case, it is first the canter itself that requires adjusting, the hindquarters may have to be either more or less loaded. If the horse changes in front before changing behind, one can canter in travers-like position before asking for the change. If on the contrary the horse changes behind first, a hint of shoulder-in position would be appropriate.

Alfred Knopfhart *Dressage A Guidebook for the Road to Success*

Paul Belasik analyses the different factors that may cause late changes behind and in front, and suggests remedial action for each:

If the horse is late behind, it usually means that the rider needs more activity to shorten the length of the hind leg steps and quicken the step. It will be much easier for the horse to make a small jump than a big one. Then, after the horse has learned the change, the rider can open the canter up again. If the horse is late in front, it usually means that it is getting caught by the reins. The rider has to make sure that the neck is not locked stiff, not by bending it, but by encouraging it to reach straight into

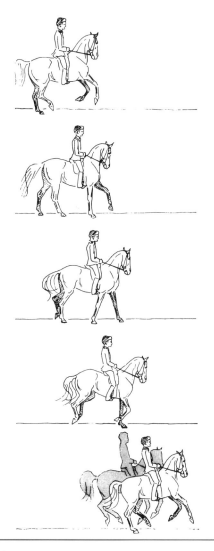

*Incorrect flying change; split change in left canter, from Alfred Knopfhart's* Dressage A Guidebook for the Road to Success.

the new turn. It is very important not to bend the horse to signal the change. If you bend the neck and head into the new change, this will come back to haunt you later when you try to make straight tempi changes.

Paul Belasik  *Dressage for the 21st Century*

The faults of crooked or swinging changes are addressed by John Winnett:

Most of the time when I encounter this problem, it is on horses already trained in flying changes by other people. Again, the horse's rectitude must be considered, together with weaknesses in basic training. I have had good results correcting this problem by using the wall of the hall to help restrain the side-to-side swing, and riding the changes as forward as possible. The increased tempo and impulsion force the hind legs more forward under the horse and keep him straighter. I also emphasise the stronger use of my inside leg at the girth, and a lot of counter-canter along the wall.

John Winnett  *Dressage as Art in Competition*

Knopfhart, agreeing with Winnett about the use of the inside leg, also warns against inappropriate use of the outside leg...

Swaying of the croup, amounting sometimes to just plain crookedness, is usually due to insufficient driving effect of the inside leg, or to predominant use of the outside leg. If it occurs only to one side, it is probably because the natural one-sidedness of the horse has not been corrected...

...adding:

...The hindquarters of a horse that has not been taught to canter straight cannot be controlled by the rider's legs. Straightness at the canter is the first condition of correct execution of the changes.

Alfred Knopfhart *Dressage A Guidebook for the Road to Success*

This correlation between the rider's leg aids and straightness – or lack of it – in canter, is addressed by Paul Belasik, who refers to the potential for problems in flying changes if early aids to canter are not given with due precision.

It is very important to make these initial strike-offs as straight as possible by using *both* legs and by not using the outside leg too strongly, since this will push the hindquarters sideways.

Let me give you an example of a very common advanced problem that begins at this very early stage. Later...the horse will have been trained in shoulder-in, haunches-in, renvers, and half-pass. If you will, all of these exercises are purposely-crooked exercises. The horse will move its hindquarters at the slightest hint of unilateral leg pressure. Eventually, it becomes time to

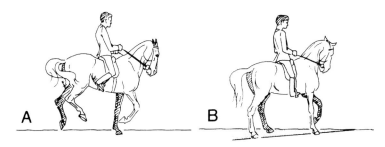

*Incorrect flying change:* **A** = *Lifting of the croup;* **B** = *Deviation with the hindquarters.*

*Incorrect flying change from Alfred Knopfhart's* Dressage A Guidebook for the Road to Success.

teach the tempi flying changes. But this particular horse was trained to strike-off into the canter from the signal of the outside leg. As the rider changes from one strong outside leg aid to the other, he can't understand why the changes are not straight! Therefore, the rider must take care not only to keep the leg pressure more even, but also to accustom the horse to follow the rider's hip and center of gravity, or weight aids, for direction. In the canter strike-off, both legs create impetus while a slight, asymmetrical shift of weight signals the lead. The rider...brings the right hip (in this example [for right lead]) forward, without twisting the upper body, and the horse learns to bring its right hip forward also. So, although the canter is signaled in part by the rider's outside leg, it is really a complex gesture, which must also be directed by the inside leg and by the rider's hips, which feel as though they pull the hind legs under, the inside hip being just enough in advance to govern the lead. In order to get good quality flying changes later on, these initial strike-offs must be straight, powerful and governed by the rider's weight, not by excessive lower leg aids.

Paul Belasik  *Dressage for the 21st Century*

Inappropriate leg aids are also cited by Knopfhart as one reason for croup-high changes:

If the horse lifts his croup it can be because he is not yet sufficiently master of his equilibrium, but it is often because the rider displaces his leg too far back and hits with his heel the ticklish spot on the horse's flank, or because he pulls on the reins...

Alfred Knopfhart  *Dressage A Guidebook for the Road to Success*

John Winnett focuses on problems rooted in the horse's physique and balance, and explains his remedies:

Flying changes performed with a high croup can be the result of the horse's conformation...or lack of suppleness in the hind legs. To correct this fault, I ride the changes on the diagonal in an energetic collected canter, placing as many half-halts as necessary to keep the horse from transferring his centre of gravity too far forward. I have also found it helpful to ride to the end of the diagonal, ask for a half pirouette and ride back and then make a few changes, finishing the diagonal in another half pirouette back again. The pirouettes help re-establish collection and flexion of the hind legs.

John Winnett *Dressage as Art in Competition*

He also offers a remedy for changes made over the bit:

This fault can be easily corrected by reverting to the simple changes, especially through the walk, which tend to put the horse back on the bit. Then I ask for one flying change at X on both leads until the single changes are perfect and on the bit.

John Winnett *Dressage as Art in Competition*

In a broader equestrian context, this fault is often associated with excitement and rushing. In counteracting these problems, Fillis makes the simple observation:

If the horse gets excited I stop him, but I do not pat him, for, if I did so, he might think that I was encouraging him to get excited. James Fillis *Breaking and Riding*

Winnett addresses rushing in tandem with anticipation, the two often being related:

Rushing and anticipating. Sometimes backing off momentarily in training the changes is helpful. In general, I have had success overcoming this problem by counter-cantering the short side of the hall to put the horse back on my aids and interrupting the lesson with many periods of walk and relaxation. Ask for little in the beginning, but ask often. When a horse anticipates the flying change, it is wise to check the straightness of neck and head. The rider must also make sure that outside leg contact remains on the horse's flank a little longer until the new change is asked for. Also, never ask for a change in the same place twice.          John Winnett *Dressage as Art in Competition*

**Fillis expressed a marked preference for high-spirited Thoroughbreds, and it is not entirely clear whether the following reference is to anticipation as such, or to unilateral decisions on the part of the horses he rode. What is of significance is that his 'punishment' is really a check or correction; that it is balanced by reward and he does not continue with the exercise at a time when doing so might cause confusion or confrontation.**

It happens with all horses, that when they have learned to do the changes easily, they will do them of their own accord, and without an indication from the rider. In this case the horse should be punished, because if we let him take the initiative, we can get no regularity in the changes.

When I say...punished, I mean that the fault ought to be checked. Thus, if when the horse is cantering on the off fore, he changes before we ask him to do so, he should simply be touched more sharply than usual with the left spur, in order to oblige him to rest on the right leg...Having checked the fault in the manner...indicated, we should avoid again requiring a change of leg in the air during the same lesson, as it might confuse the horse...

If we have checked the same fault several times and have

taken care to pat the animal when he changes only when we have asked him, he will soon understand...But, I repeat, we should do the changes only when we have not been obliged to punish the animal. It is better to devote several lessons to checking the fault, in which case the horse will understand much better, will be quieter, and his breaking will be more rapid.               James Fillis  *Breaking and Riding*

Whilst pointing out the value of careful observation and some initial repetition when starting the changes, Knopfhart warns against continuing the latter to a degree which might engender anticipation. He also brings up the topic of one-sidedness.

...When one begins to teach the lesson, one must carefully observe to which side, at what place and at what speed the horse changes most easily. The place must be changed as soon as the horse reacts satisfactorily to the aids and also if he antic-ipates the indications of the rider. On the other hand, if he con-tinually declines to change to one side, this will always be the 'stiff' side, and clearly indicates marked one-sidedness and unequal contact which must be corrected before proceeding with the lesson.

   Alfred Knopfhart  *Dressage A Guidebook for the Road to Success*

Despite progressive training, some residual degree of one-sidedness persists in most horses and, as in other exercises, it will be evident in the flying changes. Acknowledging this, Winnett prescribes further attention to the suppling exercises aimed at correcting it:

Most horses will change leads with more ease from right to left, so it is best to start asking for the first change from the right rein. If the horse shows great difficulty in changing from left to right, we must pause to examine the cause. Most of the time it is a fault of rectitude. If the horse in question is dominant on his right lateral, he will canter with greater ease on his left lead…When this fault occurs and persists, the best correction is back to the basic lateral suppling exercises in the trot and perfecting the counter-canter.

John Winnett  *Dressage as Art in Competition*

Belasik suggests, also, that the 'difficult' change can be isolated and improved:

Another problem is that the changes are uneven, left and right, or one is larger and/or freer than the other: these are proofs of asymmetry. The faulty side and the change have to be isolated and improved. Let us say, for example, that the change from right to left is not of the same quality as the change from left to right. The rider can take the horse to the rail or the wall, pick up the counter-canter on the right lead, continue until the balance feels fairly good, and make a flying change to the left. Now, the rider should not do a flying change back to the right – that change is fine. Instead, the procedure is to make a simple change, or a transition down to walk or trot. If the horse feels a little strong, the rider should definitely return to the walk and wait until the horse settles. When the horse feels about right (probably not perfect – the rider who waits for perfection won't get in any practice), the rider must resume the right lead counter-canter, balance it, make it very straight and then change again. The whole process is then repeated, the idea being to continue isolating the faulty change in order to polish it.

Paul Belasik  *Dressage for the 21st Century*

Finally, on the subject of faults and difficulty, there are warnings that over-reaction by the rider will simply serve to exacerbate them; problems must be kept in perspective and dealt with patiently:

Flying changes are relatively quick and subtle. When small problems arise, the rider has to be careful not to get consumed by them. A strong reaction by the rider can set up suspicion or anxiety in the horse, thus engendering a real problem of confidence where before none existed. A strong physical reaction almost always pushes the horse sideways, thus making it crooked. In principle, this is rather like getting after a horse excessively for shying. The horse becomes afraid of and/or anticipates the punishment, as well as the source of the shying: the whole process doubles the anxiety. However, if the basics are followed, in a year or so the horse will grow out of the problem. When faced with such difficulties, a rider who really cares about the training of horses and equestrian practice must constantly remember not to panic.

Paul Belasik  *Dressage for the 21st Century*

Each time I have any difficulty in the changes…I go back to starting at the canter [**transitions to canter**]. The starts are for the horse, what scales are for pianists…

James Fillis  *Breaking and Riding*

## *Developing Sequence Changes*

The sequence changes are a prime example of the need for measured progression in training, and of the rewards for adhering to this practice. Among the Masters, there is a considerable consensus that it is relatively easy to introduce the horse to the concept of sequence changes, *provided that the single changes are correct and have been properly established.*

Before demanding changes of lead at close intervals, single changes of lead must first be perfected. It would, of course, be absurd to hope that changes of lead at close intervals would be done with ease as long as single changes are not done perfectly... André Jousseaume *Progressive Dressage*

The repeated flying changes, including the changes *a tempo*, are (granted that the horse has learnt to understand the rider's intention), more a test of the rider's adroitness than of the horse's athletic prowess. They do not demand particularly pronounced hock flexion; on the contrary, the less the horse is set on the haunches, the more easily he can do the changes.

Kurt Albrecht     *Principles of Dressage*

A well-trained horse that is instantly sensitive to the slightest indication of the hand and leg can be made to change regularly every third or second stride and a co-operative horse can be trained to change the leading leg every stride at the canter. But before reaching this stage the closest co-operation must exist between horse and rider and any change made must be executed smoothly and precisely...

Geoffrey Brooke  *Horsemanship Dressage & Show-Jumping*

If the horse manifests no excitement during a single flying change, and its even loading on all four legs remains unimpaired, the only factors controlling its training in several successive changes after a certain number of strides are the degree of supple responsiveness achieved and the methodical training during exercise.

If difficulties arise…we must always return to the simpler exercise.            Waldemar Seunig *Horsemanship*

To obtain successive changes without difficulty or disadvantages, the single changes must be equally easy on both leads… However, even more than their perfection, it is their symmetry that matters and the absolute evenness of their rhythm and length.          General Decarpentry *Academic Equitation*

When the rider can obtain a single flying change anywhere in the arena, when it is straight, and when the horse waits for the rider to change with the seat, then the horse is ready to begin multiple changes and tempi changes.

Paul Belasik   *Dressage for the 21st Century*

Writing of early work on sequence changes, Belasik points out that consistent practise on the rider's part is a key factor in achieving the requisite degree of co-operation by the horse:

At this point the intervals between changes are unimportant. What is important is that the horse waits for the rider. If, when the changes were started, they were always set up, that habit will pay off. If there is no habitual set-up, there will be no change. The rider should always prepare for the changing and should never surprise the horse.

Paul Belasik   *Dressage for the 21st Century*

Nuno Oliveira also emphasises the need for correct preparation and use of the aids:

Procedures to obtain flying changes close together are no different. The important thing is the way in which the aids are used, the degree of preparation, and the position given to the horse.

It is necessary to proceed calmly in order to come to the point when flying changes at every stride may be demanded, after having ensured flying changes when asked for every sixth, fifth, third and second stride. Only then, when the others are definite, should flying changes at every stride be tried.

Nuno Oliveira  *Reflections on Equestrian Art*

When flying changes are demanded close together in sequence, it is essential to have the same contact in both reins otherwise the changes will never be straight. The more you ask in close sequence, the more you must ensure the cadence.

Nuno Oliveira  *Notes and Reminiscences of a Portuguese Rider*

Jousseaume, also, highlights the need for straightness in the horse and precision in the rider:

Seek precision, by setting points in advance...The rider should confine himself to demanding the change of lead only at the point he has fixed in advance. He will thus be forced to prepare his horse in time, and this will result in precision not only on the part of the horse, but also the rider. Both will approach perfection, one in the execution, the other in the demand...

In this work, seek the same degree of lightness and precision as in the single changes of lead. As soon as the horse places his weight on the forehand...adjust his equilibrium with half-halts, for the lack of lightness comes from a change in balance which takes place during...the change of lead...

The question of a straight horse becomes of primary importance, because the horse must always be in a position to go from one lead to the other.

André Jousseaume  *Progressive Dressage*

**While Seunig comments:**

Changes of lead after several successive gallops should be exercised only along a straight line, away from the wall, or along the line from one side of the riding hall to the other, so that the rider can clearly see how much of the horse's straightness is attributable to its obedience to the controls and be sure that the horse is kept from growing accustomed to moral support from the wall.

Waldemar Seunig *Horsemanship*

**The Masters also offer caveats against rider error...**

Obtaining successive lead changes without difficulty depends entirely to what extent the single lead change has been perfected...

With respect to successive lead changes, one must avoid twisting the upper body or moving from one buttock to the other. Unfortunately, the rider is all too often inclined to make these movements which disrupt the harmony that he must maintain with his horse...

Alexis-François L'Hotte *Questions Équestres* (in *Alexis-François L'Hotte The Quest For Lightness In Equitation,* by Hilda Nelson)

**...and impatience:**

The moment we are satisfied that the horse will give us a change whenever we ask for it, we can start him at changing his leg at regular intervals of a given number of strides. It is best to begin very easily, say with one change in every twenty or even thirty strides. Gradually we may then reduce the number of intervening strides until the horse can change after every eight or ten...Then we must not, for a time, reduce the number of strides any further...We must...first of all, make absolutely sure that the horse changes to our aids, and not by any change from intuition. To that end, we shall make him change at irregular intervals...

When we are satisfied that the horse has thoroughly understood and changes with precision every time that we apply the aids, we may gradually increase our demands...

Henry Wynmalen *Equitation*

**After describing continued steady progress, Wynmalen emphasises the need for adroitness and correct timing on the rider's part, if the changes at close intervals are to be correct and clean:**

I do not consider the change at every third stride unduly difficult, since the rider has time to sit still while the horse takes two complete strides...but to obtain the change at every two strides the rider has only one complete stride between the reversal of his aids...And finally for the change at every stride, the rider has no time at all between the changes, but must reverse his aids continuously; thus while the horse swings his off-fore out the rider must simultaneously apply the reversed aid for the near-fore to lead, and vice versa...When a man walks his right arm swings back while his right leg swings forward. It has always struck me, when riding a change of leg at every stride, that it is as if the horse were a walking man, using my legs as a man would his arms*. And that is perhaps the clearest way of explaining this very difficult movement.

[*One interprets this as an illustration, not an indication that the rider's legs should swing markedly.]

Henry Wynmalen *Equitation*

**Wynmalen's remarks about the one-time changes take us back to the concept that many authorities still see a distinction**

between even close-sequence changes and the one-time changes. Whereas Alfred Knopfhart views the sequence changes in general as quite straightforward, he warns that the horse's inherent capacity will always be a factor where one-time changes are concerned:

Once correct isolated flying changes to both sides are well established and can be performed also from counter-canter to counter-canter, it is time to proceed with the changes after a given number of strides. No further explanation is necessary; the principles remain the same. It remains a matter of progressiveness and one should expect few hitches. The flying changes at every stride are the crowning achievement, but there are horses who will always remain incapable of really mastering them.

Alfred Knopfhart  *Dressage A Guidebook for the Road to Success*

As we saw in the section on Historical Development, John Winnett appears to have some reservations about the underlying principle of one-time changes ('I often wonder whether the exercise of flying changes at every stride is art or circus!'). In practical terms, however, he adopts a very positive view of their introduction:

Teaching the changes at every stride is relatively easy. First I assume that my changes every second stride are perfected; straight, forward, clean and on the bit. At this stage, I will take the counter-canter (usually right) and ask for one change every stride: right – left. Immediately upon success, I reward and walk, and start again. After a few days, when the horse is confirmed in the single change along the wall; right left and left, right, I then progress to the frontier of the problem – every stride: right – left – right. When the horse can perform these three changes at every stride on both reins, it will be fairly easy to obtain five. At this point, I start asking for the changes on the diagonals, and usually from here on it will be very easy to obtain as many successive changes as I want.

However, this is tempered by a warning that there may be some time-lapse between the horse's understanding of the movement, and his ability to perform it to his full potential:

What takes the utmost patience is not asking the horse to cover more ground per stride than he can give. Some horses take many months of training before they establish the balance and timing they need to show their fullest potential, which must be long, ground-covering, flying leaps, performed in a very forward canter.     John Winnett *Dressage as Art in Competition*

It may be appropriate to leave the final word on one-time changes to Gustav Steinbrecht, whose famous maxim 'Ride your horse forward and set it straight' must lie at the very heart of success in this movement.

Slow and systematic progress on the correct basis is the most reliable way to arrive at one's goal. If one remains faithful to these principles, as should be a matter of course for the true expert, and the physical talents of the horse permit it, one will finally arrive at a point where the flying changes can be performed at every stride. However, such changes can be considered proper dressage movements only if they are performed precisely on a straight forward line without any noticeable aids from the rider, particularly without any non-equestrian and unsightly throwing of the upper body from side to side as is unfortunately seen very frequently today.

Gustav Steinbrecht *The Gymnasium of the Horse*

*'If the basics have been mastered, the changes should be so straight that one could roll a ball down a straight line between the horse's legs.'*
*Photo sequence from Paul Belasik's* Dressage for the 21st Century.

# Conclusion

In counter-canter and the flying change we see two movements that are of considerable use to the rider – the former primarily for its gymnastic value, the latter partly for its practical value in various disciplines and partly as a demonstration of human and equine adroitness and rapport. This quality of rapport is, in fact, an essential ingredient in the successful introduction and practice of both movements: in addition to an understanding of their mechanics, both require considerable equestrian tact on the part of the rider.

However valuable counter-canter may be as a gymnastic exercise, it is still a form of movement that is contrary to the horse's basic instincts, and it may be instructive to reiterate Wynmalen's analysis and strictures in this respect:

We now want him to understand that he must give up acting in accordance with his own sense of balance and that he must in future submit to our judgment in the matter...

It is not difficult to succeed in this at the appropriate stage of the horse's training, but it does require tact; it is...an exercise in which we can only succeed by explaining to the horse's brain and not by acting forcibly on his anatomy.

Henry Wynmalen *Dressage A Study of the Finer Points of Riding*

So far as the flying changes are concerned, we have seen that their introduction is not always straightforward and that progress should never be rushed. These concepts are encapsulated in the words of James Fillis...

If we go too fast we will not succeed, for the horse cannot help making mistakes...By going quietly in riding, we shall be certain of succeeding quickly. Besides, the horse is the one who indicates to us the number of changes and the interval between them without spoiling his equilibrium, strength, or lightness.

James Fillis  *Breaking and Riding*

...and John Winnett...

Finally, I would like to say that it is best not to ask for too much too fast in training flying changes. It is best to work changes only on days when we schedule their training, and to be content with the slightest progress. Start with a fresh horse and end the session on a happy note. Never tire the horse by asking more than he can give...

John Winnett  *Dressage as Art in Competition*

...which are evidence of a philosophy that should permeate all equestrian exercises.

# Bibliography

Many of the books cited in this work have been produced in numerous editions, sometimes by more than one publisher. Some, indeed, have been subject to various translations into different languages. Listed below are the editions which have been referred to during the compilation of this book. Where appropriate, information on first publication has been added, to help place the works in historical context.

Albrecht, Kurt, *Principles of Dressage*, J. A. Allen (London) 1993. (1st edn. Verlag ORAC, Vienna 1981).

Baucher, François, *New Method of Horsemanship*, in *François Baucher the Man and his Method*, Hilda Nelson, J. A. Allen (London) 1992. (First published as *Méthode d'Equitation basée sur de nouveaux principes*, France 1842.)

Belasik, Paul, *Riding Towards the Light*, J. A. Allen (London) 1990. *Dressage for the 21st Century*, J. A. Allen (London) 2002.

Burger, Üdo, *The Way to Perfect Horsemanship* (tr. Nicole Bartle), J. A. Allen (London) 1998. (First published as *Vollendete Reitkunst*, Paul Parey, Berlin and Hamburg 1959.)

Brooke, Maj.-Gen. Geoffrey, *Horsemanship Dressage & Show-Jumping*, Seeley, Service & Co. Ltd. (London) 1968 (1st edn. 1929).

Decarpentry, Gen., *Academic Equitation* (tr. Nicole Bartle),

J. A. Allen (London) 1987. (First published in France 1949).

De la Guérinière, François Robichon, *School of Horsemanship* (tr. Tracy Boucher), J. A. Allen (London) 1994. (First published in a single volume as *Ecole de Cavalerie*, Paris 1733.)

Fillis, James, *Breaking and Riding*, J. A. Allen (London) 1986. (1st English edn 1902.)

Herbermann, Erik, *Dressage Formula* (3rd edn.), J. A. Allen (London) 1999.

Jousseaume, André, *Progressive Dressage* (tr. Jeanette Vigneron), J. A. Allen (London) 1978. (First published in France by Émile Hazan.)

Knopfhart, Alfred, *Dressage A Guidebook for the Road to Success*, Half Halt Press, Inc., (Maryland) 1996.

L'Hotte, Gen. Alexis-François, *Questions Équestres* tr. Hilda Nelson in *Alexis-François L'Hotte The Quest For Lightness In Equitation*, J. A. Allen (London) 1997. (*Questions Équestres* first published in France, 1906.)

Nelson, Hilda, *François Baucher the Man and his Method*, J. A. Allen (London) 1992.

Oliveira, Nuno, *Reflections on Equestrian Art* (tr. Phyllis Field), J. A. Allen (London) 1988. (First published as *Reflexions sur l'Art Equestre*, Crépin Leblond, France 1964.)

*Notes and Reminiscences of a Portuguese Rider*, special publication 1982.

Podhajsky, Alois, *My Horses, My Teachers* (tr. Eva Podhajsky), J. A. Allen (London) 1997. (First published as *Meine Lehrmeister die Pferde*, Nymphenburger Verlagshandlung GmbH., Munich 1968.)

*The Complete Training of Horse and Rider* (tr. Eva Podhajsky), The Sportsman's Press (London) 1997. (First published as *Die Klassiche Reitkunst*, Nymphenburger Verlagshandlung GmbH., Munich 1965.)

Seunig, Waldemar, *Horsemanship* (tr. Leonard Mins), Robert Hale (London) 1958. (First published in Germany 1941.)

*The Essence of Horsemanship* (tr. Jacqueline Stirlin Harris), J. A. Allen (London) 1986. (First published in Germany by Erich Hoffmann Verlag 1961.)

Steinbrecht, Gustav, *The Gymnasium of the Horse* (tr. from German 10th edn. Helen K. Buckle), Xenophon Press (Ohio) 1995. (First published in Germany 1885.)

Wätjen, Richard L., *Dressage Riding* (tr. Dr V. Saloschin), J. A. Allen (London) 1973. (First published in Germany 1958.)

Winnett, John, *Dressage as Art in Competition*, J. A. Allen (London) 1993.

Wynmalen, Henry, *Dressage A Study of the Finer Points of Riding*, Wilshire Book Company (California). (First published in 1952.)

*Equitation*, J. A. Allen (London) 1971. (1st edn.1938.)

# Biographies of Quoted Masters

The following are brief biographies of those whose works are cited in this book. They are given both for reasons of general interest and to assist the reader in placing each author in historical and cultural context.

**Albrecht, Kurt** Born in Austria in 1920, Albrecht chose a military career and saw active service as an Artillery Commander in the Second World War, before becoming a prisoner of war in Russia. After the war, he joined the Austrian Constabulary and taught equitation at the Constabulary Central School.

Albrecht was a great friend of Hans Handler and, when Handler succeeded Alois Podhajsky as Director of the Spanish Riding School, Albrecht joined the School to assist with administration, being appointed Substitute Director in 1965. In 1974 he succeeded Handler as Director, a post he held until 1985.

From 1973 until 1987 Albrecht was in charge of judges' affairs for the Austrian Equestrian Federation, subsequently playing a leading role in equestrian educational advancement.

**Baucher, François** (1796–1873) A highly controversial figure, who rode entirely in the school, Baucher began his career under the tutelage of his uncle, director of stables to the Governor of

Milan. Whilst in Italy, he would have witnessed the practices of the old Neapolitan school, which were still dominant in that country.

In 1816, political upheaval saw Baucher's return to France, where he managed and taught in several private manèges. In 1834, he moved to Paris and established a relationship with the fashionable Franconi circus. Riding haute école in the circus gave Baucher the prestige he yearned, and in 1842 he published his 'new method' *(Méthode d'Equitation basée sur de nouveaux principes)*.

In 1855, Baucher was badly injured when the chandelier of an indoor school fell on him. Thereafter, he never performed in public again, although he remained able to do some riding and teaching. In later life, he became very reflective and appears to have modified some of his earlier ideas.

The controversy that surrounded Baucher's writing and teaching is well documented in Hilda Nelson's *François Baucher the Man and his Method*, in which the author writes: 'The goal of Baucher's method is the total disposition of the horse's strength and the total submission of the horse to the will of the horseman.' What is beyond question is that Baucher trained a number of dangerous horses to perform advanced movements in a remarkably short time, and Fillis said of him: 'He had the great merit of not describing anything which he could not do.'

Baucher remains respected by many eminent authorities and his reputation is believed by some to have been compromised by equestrian politics, the limitations of his own powers of expression, and the insensitivity of his translators.

**Belasik, Paul** Born in Buffalo, New York in 1950, Belasik showed a strong affinity with animals from childhood. Early interests included monkey breeding and falconry, as well as horses. This diversity of interest extended beyond the animal kingdom – entering Cornell University as part of the pre-veterinary programme, he graduated with a science degree and had, in the meantime, won prizes for his painting and become a published poet.

By the time of his graduation in 1971, Belasik's career as a horseman had already begun; he taught college courses, evented and competed in dressage at all levels. However, never really excited by competition, he began to focus more on an in-depth study of equitation for its own sake. Initially involved in breeding and training German horses, he focused first upon the German system, broadening and deepening his studies to encompass the different schools of riding. He cites as major influences H.L.M. van Schaik, who instilled in him a love of the classicists and Nuno Oliveira, with whom he spent some time in Portugal. His interest in the philosophical aspects of equitation has been augmented by studies of Zen Buddhism and the martial arts.

Belasik owns and operates a training stable in Pennsylvania, where he works with a broad-based clientele including international competitors, and riders of all levels who have no interest in competition. He also holds clinics and lectures on a national and international basis.

**Burger, Üdo** (1914–1980) One of Germany's most respected veterinary surgeons and animal psychologists, Burger was an accomplished horseman and a highly respected judge. Involved with horses from an early age, he was reputed to become fretful if unable to spend some time each day in their company. Very obviously a horse lover, he wrote (without giving specific detail) that a horse had actually saved his life in wartime. His professional skills gave him a profound understanding of both the horse's movement and motivation, and he could be blunt in his criticism of rough riding, and of those who made insufficient effort to understand the horse's nature.

**Brooke, Maj.-Gen. Geoffrey** (1884–1966) Brooke was a genuine all-round horseman. His book *Horsemanship Dressage & Show-Jumping* includes chapters on racing over fences and polo. As a Lt. Colonel he was, in the 1920s, Chief Instructor to the British Cavalry School at Weedon, at a time when British equitation was undergoing a modernising transformation under European influences. A keen student of equitation, he might fairly be described as one of the figures who helped to move British equitation forward.

**Decarpentry, General** (1878–1956) Born at Lambres, the son and grandson of enthusiastic pupils of François Baucher, Decarpentry soon decided upon a career in the cavalry. Wounded in action at Verdun, he dismissed the permanent damage to his left elbow, saying that it kept his arm bent in the correct position for riding. The injury had no adverse affect on his career, since he was to become commander of cavalry at Saint-Cyr and second in command of the Cadré Noir (1925–31).

From 1939 onward, Decarpentry acted as judge at many international dressage competitions. He also presided over the FEI jury and became President of the FEI Dressage Committee, in which role he was highly influential in developing an international consensus on the aims and judging of competition dressage.

As a rider and equestrian thinker, Decarpentry was by no means confined by the Baucheriste influences of his childhood, as both the references cited in *Academic Equitation*, and his own text shows. It is also evident that he took innovative advantage of the then-young techniques of cinematography to help analyse equine movement.

Decarpentry was a modest man and, although held in great esteem as a rider, he had no desire to participate in competition, his legacy being the skill of his instruction, his work in developing the FEI and the integrity and scholarship which he applied to his equestrian writing.

**De la Guérinière, François Robichon** (c.1688–1751) Widely regarded as the most influential figure in equestrian history, de la Guérinière was born in Essay, the son of a lawyer. A pupil of Antoine de Vendeuil, he also had a brother who ran a riding academy in Caen. In 1715, de la Guérinière was granted the title of *écuyer de roi*, and opened a riding academy in Paris, apparently under licence from the Duc d'Anjou.

At his Parisian academy, de la Guérinière taught not only riding, but what was described as 'the complete science of the horse'. By 1730 his reputation was such that he was given the Directorship of the Académie des Tuileries. Despite phenomenal success as a teacher, de la Guérinière was unable to run the academy profitably, and struggled constantly with money – a fact which might endear him to modern-day equestrians.

De la Guérinière's legacy was to develop, from the older style of classical riding, a freedom of movement which characterises modern classical equitation – an achievement which has led him to be described as the 'first of the modern classical riders' (W.S.Felton) and 'undoubtedly the father of modern equitation' (Wynmalen). His lucid work *Ecole de Cavalerie* is quite remarkable for its timeless relevance and wisdom, and continues to be a source of reference for many present-day authorities.

**Fillis, James** (1834–1913) Born in London, Fillis went to France at an early age. There he met François Baucher and, greatly impressed by his methods, studied them under Baucher's pupil,

François Caron. (Later in life, Fillis found himself at odds with some of Baucher's ideas – as his Commentaries on Baucher in *Breaking and Riding* show – but he always retained an overall admiration for him.)

After running his own school in Le Havre, Fillis moved to Paris, where he supervised the stables of various members of the nobility. Then, wishing to promote his method more widely, he followed the same course as Baucher, and began to perform in the circus, to great acclaim. Pressed to produce a book, Fillis was offered editorial assistance by a long-time pupil, the French politician, Clemenceau. Published in 1890, the book was subsequently translated into English by the eminent veterinary author, Horace Hayes.

From 1891–7, Fillis was based in Germany. He then went to Russia with Circus Ciniselli and created such an impression that he was offered, and accepted, the post of Colonel and Ecuyer-en-chef of the Russian Cavalry School – a position he held until retiring in 1910. During his period of office, a visiting American Army Commission decided to adopt his method, and *Breaking and Riding* became the official textbook of the US Cavalry School.

Interestingly, given that he was active only a century ago, Fillis totally disapproved of women riding astride!

**Herbermann, Erik** Born in Amsterdam in 1945. Herbermann moved, at an early age with his family to Johannesburg and ten years later, moved to Canada. His initial equestrian training was with Patricia Salt FBHS, herself a pupil of Richard Wätjen and Oberbereiter Lindenbauer at the Spanish Riding School. Herbermann subsequently studied under the celebrated classical riding teacher, Egon von Neindorff.

Now residing in the USA, Herbermann devotes much of his

time to lecturing, teaching and conducting clinics internationally. As well as producing three editions of *Dressage Formula*, he has also written numerous articles for equestrian publications.

Herbermann is a staunch advocate of classical ideals, and his ideology is based on an objective study of the horse's nature, which seeks the depth of understanding and quality of work perceived in the greatest of Renaissance Masters. In common with these luminaries, he views equitation as a self-improving art, rooted in the utmost affection and respect for the horse.

**Jousseaume, André** (d. 1960) A graduate of Saumur and a cavalry officer for most of his lifetime, Jousseaume won the individual silver medal for dressage at the 1932 Olympics when a member of the French gold medal winning team, and repeated this feat in both respects in 1948. He also took the bronze medal in 1952. He retired from the French army with the rank of Colonel and taught at the *Cercle Hippique* until his death.

**Knopfhart, Alfred** Born in Vienna in 1927, Knopfhart studied economics and business administration, graduating in these subjects in 1951. Having begun riding in Austria at the age of nineteen, he then went to Germany to continue his equestrian studies. In 1962 he became a certified teacher of riding, and was awarded the German silver medal for riders. Since that time, he has worked continually as a trainer of horses and riders at all levels up to Grand Prix and, since 1989, has given annual clinics at several dressage centres in the USA.

In 1964, Knopfhart became a certified judge for dressage, showjumping and eventing; in 1968 an official of the Austrian Horse Show Association and in 1970 an international FEI dressage judge. From 1986–96, he headed the official body of Austrian show judges.

In addition to lecturing at the University of Veterinary Medicine, Vienna, Knopfhart has written three books and many articles on equestrian issues.

**L'Hotte, Gen. Alexis-François** (1825–1904) A son and grand-son of French cavalrymen, L'Hotte was, from an early age, a keen student of the equestrian writings of the old French Masters – much to the detriment of his academic education. He initially attended the military academy of Saint Cyr as a young cadet, being sent on to pursue his equestrian interests at Saumur, since the cavalry section at Saint-Cyr had been closed. Despite some youthful indiscipline, he eventually attained the rank of General, and became Commandant of the re-opened cavalry section at Saint-Cyr, and subsequently of Saumur.

It is of great interest to students of equestrian history that L'Hotte was a pupil of both François Baucher and Comte D'Aure, two highly influential figures who not only practised different styles of equitation, but were considered rivals and had their own factions of supporters. L'Hotte was a great note-taker, and his anecdotes about and comparisons of these two figures make fascinating reading.

L'Hotte himself was considered to be one of the most out stand-ing *écuyers* of a golden age: he originated the phrase 'equestrian tact' and the famous maxim 'calm, forward and straight.'

**Nelson, Hilda** Emeritus Professor of French Civilization and Literature at San Diego State University, Hilda Nelson is a keen rider with a profound understanding of classical equestrian principles. The author of several books on her wider field of study, Professor Nelson has also translated Antoine de Pluvinel's *Le Maneige Royal* into English, and produced two important equestrian works *François Baucher the Man and his Method*, and

*Alexis-François L'Hotte The Quest For Lightness In Equitation,* which deal with the life and times of two of the key figures of nineteenth century equitation. In addition to containing translations of Baucher's *New Method of Horsemanship* and L'Hotte's *Questions Équestres* respectively, these works include highly detailed and authoritative commentaries by Professor Nelson, which will be of great value and interest to all students of equitation.

**Oliveira, Nuno** (d.1989) This great Portuguese Master began his career as a pupil of Joaquin Gonzales de Miranda, former Master of the Horse to the Portuguese Royal Family. After Miranda's death, Oliveira trained horses first for cavalry officers and a dealer, then for one of Miranda's pupils, Senōr Chefalenez. Subsequently, a friend and student, Manual de Barros asked him to train at his brother-in-law's stud where, in addition to having many good horses to ride, he also had at his disposal a large equestrian library. During this period, he met Alois Podhajsky when they both rode at an exhibition in the Campo Grande and the pair became firm friends.

During the 1950s, Oliveira attracted a number of highly talented pupils, and opened his riding school at Quinta do Chafaris. He also began to write articles (and subsequently, books) on equitation, while a pupil organised a weekly TV programme showing his lessons.

In 1961 he gave his first exhibition abroad, in Switzerland, and the following year he rode in the Winter Circus in Paris, where he met and established a lasting relationship with Capt. Durand, later to be Commander of the Cadre Noir.

Subsequent years saw a further influx of pupils, many from abroad, and numerous clinics and exhibitions throughout Europe, North and South America and Australia, which continued up to the time of his death.

**Podhajsky, Alois** (1899–1973) The son of an Austro-Hungarian cavalry officer, Podhajsky joined a dragoon regiment aged seventeen and received regular lessons from Capt. Count Telekei, whom he described as an excellent instructor.

Although in a cavalry regiment, Podhajsky spent much of the First World War on foot. After the war, following the demise of the Austro-Hungarian Empire, he was admitted to the new Federal Army, and riding once again became part of his career. Having achieved considerable success in showjumping, he was encouraged by his colonel to study dressage, which he found further improved his horse's jumping. Transferred to advanced training at the cavalry school at Schlosshof, he began to achieve international success in dressage, showjumping and three-day events.

In 1933, he was sent to the Spanish Riding School, where he studied under luminaries such as Polak, Zrust and Lindenbauer. Their influence helped him to train his own horses to Grand Prix level and to win a bronze medal for dressage at the 1936 Olympics.

From 1934–8 he worked as a cavalry instructor, first in Austria and then in Germany. In 1938 Austria was annexed by Germany, and the Spanish Riding School was placed under the command of the German Army. When, in 1939, Podhajsky became Director of the Spanish Riding School, he managed to convince senior German officers, who were experienced horsemen, of the value of the School. By this, and other actions in that period, Podhajsky was instrumental in protecting the School for posterity.

In the post-war years, Podhajsky competed abroad both with his own horses and the School's Lipizzaners. He also took the Spanish Riding School on a number of foreign tours, including a major tour of the USA shortly before his retirement in 1964.

**Seunig, Waldemar** (1887–1976) Born in the then Duchy of Krain, Seunig was educated at a military academy in Austria and entered the cavalry. He subsequently attended the Riding Instructors' Institute in Vienna, where he became a pupil of the famous Josipovich. Then, in the political upheaval of the times, he was more or less repatriated (to what was by that time Slovenia, in Yugoslavia).

Since, by then, he had established a considerable reputation, he was offered the post of Master of the Horse at the Yugoslavian Royal Court. This he accepted, on condition that he first spent a year at the French Cavalry School at Saumur, and six months at the Royal Mews in London (to learn protocol). Subsequently, he was also granted a year at the Spanish Riding School, back in Vienna.

Following a decline of royal interest in riding, Seunig became Chief Riding Master of the Yugoslavian Cavalry School in 1930. However, when offered promotion to General, he retired instead, since this would have entailed active service for a country for which he had no patriotic feelings.

After this retirement he kept riding, and, an Olympic competitor himself, also coached the German team that was successful in the Berlin Olympics. When, during the Second World War, Slovenian partisans destroyed his home, he moved to Germany where he gained high office as an equestrian instructor in the army.

After the war, he travelled extensively and became renowned as a rider, teacher and international judge. A great lover of literature, Seunig was also a keen artist and many of his own drawings adorn his books.

**Steinbrecht, Gustav** (1808–1885) Born in Saxony, Steinbrecht studied veterinary medicine before becoming a pupil of Louis

Seeger, one of the most influential trainers of the nineteent century, who had, himself, been a pupil of Weyrother, a celebrated figure of the Spanish Riding School.

Steinbrecht stayed with Seeger for eight years, during which time he married Seeger's niece and became an accomplished *écuyer*. He then took over direction of a manège in Magdeburg, where he remained for a further eight years, before rejoining Seeger.

In 1849, Steinbrecht became director of Seeger's establishment and, at about this time, began to make the notes that were to form the basis of *The Gymnasium of the Horse*. Seeger himself disagreed with the teachings of François Baucher — also active at this time — preferring methods and principles expounded by de la Guérinière. That Steinbrecht shared Seeger's view of Baucher is obvious from the vigorous attacks upon Baucher's method which permeate *The Gymnasium of the Horse*.

As Steinbrecht's health failed, he entrusted the completion of his book to his pupil/disciple, Paul Plinzner. Through Plinzner, and Plinzner's eminent pupil, Hans von Heydebreck, the work of Steinbrecht had a major influence on the formulation of the German [army] Riding Rules, and on German equitation in general.

**Wätjen, Richard L.** (b. 1891) Early backing from his parents enabled Richard Wätjen to embark upon a career devoted entirely to equitation — and he did not squander this privileged position. After studying at Trakehen and Graditz, both German government studs, he spent six years (1916–21) as a pupil of the Spanish Riding School, then stayed on for a further six years as a guest amateur instructor and trainer.

In 1925, he moved to Berlin and began training horses and riders on a professional basis. This scheme proved highly successful: his pupils achieved great national and international success, and he was instrumental in training several Olympic teams, including the British team which competed at Helsinki in 1952.

As a rider, he produced many horses of various breeds to the highest standards, and achieved international success competing in both dressage and showjumping, two of his best-known horses being Burgsdorff and Wotan. Many authorities regard him as being one of the most elegant riders of his era.

**Winnett, John** Born in Los Angeles in 1928, Winnett was educated in Paris, where he was introduced to riding in the French classical tradition by Victor Laurent, a retired officer from Saumur who had studied under the doctrine of L'Hotte. Winnett subsequently became interested in showjumping and was instructed according to the methods of Col. Danloux, who had refined principles introduced by Federico Caprilli. He became French Junior National Champion in 1945.

As an adult Winnett 'abandoned serious riding to pursue a career' in the Indian sub-continent, Europe and subsequently New York. This 'abandonment' did not prevent him from amateur race-riding, playing polo and, indeed, representing the USA in the 1952 World Showjumping Championships.

Retiring early from a successful career, Winnett turned his full concentration upon horses and went to Germany, to study with Reiner Klimke. In Germany, he was initially surprised to discover a very free-moving style of equitation which traced back to the teachings of de la Guérinière. Much influenced by these German methods, to which he added a detailed study of equine biomechanics, Winnett achieved great success in competition dressage, becoming riding captain of the American team at the 1972 Olympics and continuing to represent his country at the highest levels throughout the 1970s and 1980s.

**Wynmalen, Henry** (1889–1964) Undoubtedly one of the most influential figures in British equitation, Wynmalen was Dutch by birth and spent his early life in Holland, coming to England in 1927. An engineer by profession, Wynmalen's many interests included yachting, motor rallying and aviation. A flying accident, which left a legacy of back trouble, resulted in Wynmalen adopting a somewhat individualistic riding posture, but did not prevent him from being a consummate all-round horseman. His early years were devoted primarily to showjumping, cross-country riding and racing, and he was, for many years, MFH to the Woodland Hunt. Always concerned with the correct schooling of horses, and renowned for his quiet, patient methods, he became increasingly interested in classical dressage. In 1948, he won the British Dressage Championship, and followed this with many other successes. His displays at the Royal Windsor Show, and the ease with which his 'dressage' horses performed across country, served to ignite a greater interest in dressage in Britain – an interest he helped to promote with no reduction in his enthusiasm for the other disciplines.

A highly successful breeder and exhibitor of show horses, a respected judge and President of the Arab Horse Society, Wynmalen also served on the Executive Council of the BHS. Largely responsible for organising the horse trials competition at the 1948 (London) Olympics, he played a major role in instigating one-day events and, for some years, served as President of the Jury at Badminton horse trials.